TAKE ME HOME, TOO

More Notes on the Church Year for Children

BY PETER MAZAR
ILLUSTRATED BY CHUCK LUDEKE

I prefer to cut
children's spiritual garments
a little large,
for them to grow into,
as they will in time.
And who knows
what vivid image or hint
of the beauty of God
may remain in their mind
and memory?

Dorothy Coddington
Orate Fratres, 1949

Duplicating Duplicating ***Duplicating Pages from This Book***

The take-home notes in this book have been prepared to be photocopied onto 8½ × 11-inch paper. These notes may be duplicated by the purchaser for use by a parish or school. The copyright notice must appear on any duplicated pages. These materials may not be duplicated by any organization except a parish, school or religious community, or by anyone except the original purchaser of this book, without written permission from Liturgy Training Publications.

This book was designed by Mary Bowers. David Philippart was the editor, and Deborah Bogaert was the production editor. The book was typeset in Sabon and Univers by Kari Nicholls and James Mellody-Pizzato. Printed and bound by Rider Dickerson, Inc. of Chicago, Illinois.

ISBN 1-56854-180-5
TKHOM2

INTRODUCTION

Welcome to a second volume of **Take Me Home!** ***(The first volume, by Christine Kenny-Sheputis, is also available from Liturgy Training Publications.) The two volumes are different, yet their contents are complementary.***

The notes in these books are meant to be photocopied and handed out to students to take home. The purchase of this book gives you permission to duplicate these notes for a school or parish. There is a relevant note for every week of the year.

Take Me Home *notes can be hung on the refrigerator at home to be read and used during the week.* Artist Chuck Ludeke has included simple and beautiful illustrations that children can color. These notes can serve as reminders of special days or seasons as they approach. They can help join the liturgical life of the parish with life in our kitchens, living rooms and gardens.

The church uses the materials of this world as signs of the world to come, signs of the reign of God. We wait for the reign of God to come, yet that reign is already present among us under the signs that early Christians called "the mysteries." The church uses water and oil, bread and wine, gestures, processions, singing, proclamation and even special clothing in the liturgy at the various forms of public, communal prayer that mark Lord's Days, mornings and evenings, and when new members are baptized, two people are wed or the dead are buried.

There is also the sacramental life of the domestic church. The church celebrates at home with all kinds of materials and in all kinds of ways. Some of the most profound prayers of Christians may have the spicy aroma of a Pentecost barbecue or the taste of a Transfiguration Day picnic. A November visit to a graveyard or a visit to a tree lot during Advent can be a glimpse into heaven, a touching of eternity. And these wonders are the common property of Christians six or sixty years old, single or married, alone or in the company of others.

Here in this book you will find suggestions for prayer done by snipping evergreens, mixing cookie dough or hiding hard-boiled eggs in the backyard. Here are ideas for prayer offered while fixing supper, taking a shower or riding a bus. This is hands-on "holy play." And it is the kind of play best accomplished when all sorts of folks play together.

The language of these take-home notes is straightforward. This project was given to fourth-graders to read and comment on. Here and there, teachers and parents may need to help children with the vocabulary, and that's how any learning material should be. It was not imagined that children could make full use of *Take Me Home, Too* without cooperation from the members of their households. What is hoped is that everyone using these notes gets caught up in learning, experimentation and discovery.

These notes will enter the home as something of a challenge. Children will be bringing home a piece of paper that sometimes speaks about ovens, candles, scissors and occasionally even the spending of money. This can be a nuisance, because the notes ask parents to play an active part in the liturgical life of the home.

But not every person has a prayer life. Not every child has parents or even a home. Parents and children already may be over-taxed for time, interest or resources. These notes may not be entirely welcome without a religious educator's groundwork, advice and sensitive guidance.

Assure students and their families that these notes are not some form of required homework. They are instead springboards for household discussion, often just something to think about. Maybe every so often one of these notes will be the right thing at the right time—but not always. Urge adaptation, suggest alternatives and remain attuned to the special needs of individuals in your care.

We have tried to be practical. Author Peter Mazar has drawn these ideas from a wide range of traditions and has "kitchen tested" them in his own home. Mr. Mazar hasn't collected gimmicks here but customs worthy of celebrating the gospel.

Usually it takes years to judge the effectiveness of introducing new household customs, such as those suggested in these *Take Me Home, Too* flyers. One year, a new household custom or a new song or new form of prayer might seem foreign or even weird. The next year, it may bring vague feelings of familiarity. Then in subsequent years, the custom, song or prayer gets to be an old friend.

Children are especially quick to develop an affection for traditions.

All in all, a rich array of traditions is represented here. We have tried to include as many ethnic groups as we could, giving an emphasis to customs that transcend national divisions. Many saints' days are included. Most of the church's feast days are here, too. Because of the importance of these seasons, each week of Advent, Christmastime, Lent and Eastertime has its own page.

Some of the notes are for the same day every year, such as St. Blase's Day, which is on February 3. Some of the notes in this book cannot be dated because they deal with "movable feasts," such as Easter and the many days that depend on the date of Easter.

For some weeks there are two or more choices of handouts to be sent home. For instance, perhaps one year you would send home the entry for that particular week of the Easter season, and the next year you would send home the one for April 23 about St. George—or, you could send home both.

On the facing page of each note are a few suggestions for using that note and perhaps a brief synopsis of a season. Short calendars are included for the next few years so that you will know when a particular day falls. We also have suggested the color of paper that these notes might best be printed on. Different colored papers will help you distinguish the notes—and can make them more lively, too.

You might find it easiest to photocopy several weeks' worth of notes at one time.

Your comments and suggestions about *Take Me Home, Too* are welcome. Future editions will surely reflect readers' suggestions.

CONTENTS

PENTECOST
Milk and Honey

12 DAYS AFTER **PASSOVER**
Yom Hashoah

APRIL 23
Saint George, the Dragonslayer

MAY 15
Saints Maria and Isidore, Farmers

MEMORIAL DAY
Last Monday in May ▪
A Day of Peacemaking

SCHOOL'S OUT
Building Bridges to Heaven on Earth

JUNE 20/21
The Summer Solstice ▪
Summer and Winter, Bless the Lord!

JULY 11
Saint Benedict of Nursia

JULY 20
Elijah, Prophet of Tishbe

JULY 26
Saints Anne and Joachim ▪
The Grandparents of the Lord

AUGUST 1
Lammas Day

AUGUST 10
Saint Lawrence ▪
A Servant of God

AUGUST 15
The Assumption of Mary into Heaven ▪
The Passover of the Mother of God

AUGUST 29
The Martyrdom of John the Baptist ▪
A Day of Mourning

BACK TO **SCHOOL**
A Rite of Passage

SEPTEMBER 15
The Sorrows of Mary

SEPTEMBER 22
Jonah the Prophet ▪
A Big Fish Story

ROSH HASHANAH
To a Sweet New Year!

OCTOBER 1
Saint Thérèse of the Child Jesus ▪
The Story of a Soul

OCTOBER 15
Saint Teresa of Avila

OCTOBER 21
Saint Ursula and Her Companions

ALL HALLOWSTIDE
October 31, November 1 and 2 ▪
Trick or Treat

NOVEMBER 3
Saint Martin de Porres

NOVEMBER 9
The Dedication of the Lateran Basilica in Rome ▪
Living Stones

NOVEMBER 16 AND **17**
Margaret of Scotland and Elizabeth of Hungary ▪
Noblesse Oblige

NOVEMBER 22
Singing Saint Cecilia

THANKSGIVING
Now Thank We All Our God

CELEBRATING **A BIRTHDAY**
Happy Birthday to You!

FOR THE SICK
Get Well Soon!

MOVING TO **A NEW HOME**
Moving Day

FOR THOSE **WHO MOURN**
Blessed Are the Dead

An Introductory Handout

This may be used as the first handout to distribute when you begin using either volume of *Take Me Home*.

A good beginning is important. The start of the academic year, Advent, January or Lent makes a good starting point. But you need something more than a handout to encourage the use of *Take Me Home*. Any kind of ongoing program needs an initial pep talk and then some regular words of encouragement. On occasion, ask children and their parents how they're making use of these handouts, and then share that information with others in the church bulletin or newsletter.

TAKE ME HOME

Welcome!

Each week you'll be receiving one of these flyers to take home. That's why they're called *Take Me Home!* Attach them to the refrigerator or "household message center," where they can be read during the week. Perhaps you might gather the household to read them and figure out how to use the information.

Throughout the year, these *Take Me Home* flyers will be sharing all sorts of ways to live and celebrate the Christian faith. There will be ways to pray, a song to sing or a passage to read from the Bible. Sometimes there will be projects to try or recipes to prepare. Always there will be ideas to think and talk about.

But be warned: *Take Me Home* sometimes suggests using scissors, candles, ovens and other dangerous equipment, and on occasion there are suggestions for ways to spend a bit of money. And there's another challenge: Parents as well as children will be asked to take an active role in ritual prayer, fasting and feasting, and the practice of charity. That's a tall order!

These flyers may bring into your home the right idea at the right time, but not always. Be creative in adapting the ideas.

Take Me Home is based on tried-and-true Christian traditions. "Tradition" means "hand-me-down," something precious we receive from our ancestors. But like any hand-me-down, traditions can become tattered and worthless unless each generation alters and repairs them to suit the times. *Take Me Home* can help spark this good and necessary work as one generation hands on its traditions to the next.

First Week of Advent

Advent begins four Sundays before Christmas Day and lasts until sundown Christmas Eve, when the season of Christmas begins.

Advent is a season of expectancy and eager anticipation. It is a rehearsal for what all our days must be "as we wait in joyful hope for the coming of our Savior, Jesus Christ."

Religious educators have a special responsibility to foster Advent's spirit of waiting, patience and vigilance. Teachers have a unique charge to build up an appreciation for the spirit of the liturgy and for the church's calendar, especially when that calendar is in such contrast to the commercial propaganda that would have us celebrate Christmas weeks ahead of its time, leaving no room for Advent.

The take-home notes for Advent would be particularly attractive if photocopied on buff, purple, gray, rose or blue paper.

Excitement for the coming of Christmas is one aspect of Advent. Another aspect has to do with the hopes and fears of the Christian people. As this handout explains, the liturgy of November and December brings us an opportunity to face our fears, beginning with our fear of the dark.

1ST **WEEK** OF **ADVENT**

When the Stars Begin to Fall

In the Northern Hemisphere, during Advent the nights grow as long as they get. The dwindling of daylight gets some people thinking about the end of life and even the end of the world. Gazing at the night sky gets some people thinking about where they're heading in life. Such serious thoughts!

Wondering about the future can make us excited and eager, but it also can make us anxious and afraid. We want to feel confident about the future, but we also want to face our fears honestly and not hide from them.

Christian people try to develop a healthy attitude about the future. Every Sunday, we ask God to "protect us from all anxiety, as we wait in joyful hope for the coming of our Savior, Jesus Christ." And every year we have the season of Advent during which to explore the strange mix within ourselves of hope and fear, and of eagerness and anxiety.

During Advent you might pay close attention to the night sky. Befriend this holy darkness. Watch how the moon changes night to night. Search for meteors. Learn the names of constellations and the legends about these characters. Learn the names of the bright stars. (Did you know that most have Arabic names?)

Can you identify the planets? During the course of the year, it's possible to spot Mercury, Venus, Mars, Jupiter and Saturn. Because sunrises are so late during Advent, it's the easiest time of the year to watch the transformation of night into day. Keep your eyes, hearts and minds open to light!

Second Week of Advent

We hear about John the Baptist every year on the second and third Sundays of Advent and again on some of the Sundays in January. During the week before Christmas, the church tells the story of the conception and birth of John. A half year away from Christmas, on June 24, we celebrate a festival in honor of John's birth. (A handout for this "midsummer nativity" can be found in the first volume of *Take Me Home.*)

Like the prophet Elijah, John is one of the Bible's more mysterious characters. Christian poets and mystics have pondered long and hard about the details the gospels give about John's birth, life and martyrdom.

One of a teacher's many tasks is to become conversant in the Bible's "language of mystery" so that he or she can enable students to begin a lifelong exploration of this language. This handout focuses on a sweet mystery.

2ND **WEEK** OF **ADVENT**

A Sweet Tooth for Justice

The beginning of the Gospel of Mark tells us that John the Baptist ate locusts. One kind of "locust" is the grasshopper. Yuck! Another kind is the delicious fruit of the locust tree, called carob, a brown pod filled with small beans. Carob tastes like chocolate.

Another name for carob is "Saint John's bread." Especially during Advent, many grocery stores sell carob pods, which can be used to make candy. Keep an eye out for carob and carob-flavored candy to help remind you of John the Baptist and his sweet tooth.

The gospel also tells us that John ate honey. In his day, people thought honey had miraculous powers. They wondered how bees could make something so sweet. And why doesn't honey spoil? Some people felt sure that if they ate enough honey, they would live forever because their bodies wouldn't spoil!

Although we now know how bees change flower nectar into honey and how the high sugar content keeps it from spoiling, honey still seems a mystery—like liquid flowers. Sharing honey and honeycakes is a traditional way to wish one another a sweet new year.

John yelled at people who lived selfishly and greedily. Read Luke 3:7–18. Like a bee, John's angry words could sting. But in Christ's mystical body, when we share what we have with justice and mercy, we really are changed sweetly and mysteriously into something everlasting—like flowers into honey.

Third Week of Advent

The ideas in this handout can be adapted for the classroom. Another customary way to adapt these ideas at home or in the classroom is to have participants dress up as the figures instead of carrying the statues — a "living nativity."

The Central American custom of *Las Posadas* (Spanish for "lodgings") and other Filipino or European traditions for the pre-Christmas *novena* (Latin for "nine days") usually emphasize Mary and Joseph's search for a place of hospitality and rest. Those nine days are perfect for gathering alms and other gifts so that as many of God's people as possible are offered a share in the blessings of Christmas.

During Advent it's never a good idea to jump the gun on Christmas. Parties and other festivities should wait until students have reconvened after the Christmas break, when there are still several days of the Christmas season to celebrate.

A Homemade Christmas Pageant

Where does your nativity scene go? With straw, flowers, greenery and other decorations, make the spot beautiful. Some people make the figures or add new ones each year. If the statues aren't glued in place, you might use them as part of a "Christmas pageant" acted out over several weeks. Here's a way to do this:

December 16 or 17 is a traditional day to set up the stable with the ox and the empty manger but no other statues. Each night from then until Christmas Eve, gather the family and move the statues of Mary and Joseph and the donkey throughout the house room by room on their journey toward your "Bethlehem." Each time you move the statues, sing an Advent song, such as "O come, O come, Emmanuel."

Early on Christmas Eve, put the statues of Mary, Joseph and the donkey in the stable. Then late at night or early the next morning, place the statue of the infant Jesus in the manger. As you do this, read Luke 2:1–7 and sing "Silent night." On Christmas morning, the angels and shepherds arrive; read Luke 2:8–19 and sing "Hark! the herald angels sing."

From Christmas until Epiphany, the magi and their camels travel from room to room following the star. Each time you move them, sing "We three kings" or "O come, all ye faithful."

At Epiphany, as you read Matthew 2:1–11, the magi make their grand entrance so that your "Christmas pageant" is complete.

Fourth Week of Advent

Reserve some time for students to tell one another how their families celebrate Christmas. Put emphasis on the ways children take an active role.

Children too often have Christmas handed to them on a platter. Older children especially can have trouble accepting a passive role. They need to develop an ownership and a responsibility for helping the Christmas celebration to express generosity and a sense of benevolent mystery.

"Step outside and take a walk" (in other words, don't be afraid to be alone) is good advice for the times our seasonal gatherings get too stressful.

4TH **WEEK** OF **ADVENT**

The Meeting of Heaven and Earth

At sunset on Christmas Eve, the season of Advent ends and Christmastime begins. Heaven sweeps down on earth! Earth rises to heaven!

In order to open their hearts more fully to this holy exchange, some people take a walk outdoors. On a clear night, it's traditional to search for the appearing of the first three stars. Even a cloudy evening will offer its heavenly signs of the arrival of Christmas.

This night and the next, and again at the New Year, we can get away with all sorts of good, kind and generous behavior. Seize the moment! Go caroling. Dress up like an angel. Leave simple gifts by neighbors' doorways. And if folks knock on your door, welcome them warmly. Treat them like you're all members of one big, holy family.

It's an old custom on Christmas Eve to deck the halls with holly and other evergreens. We wait until now because we want the greens at their fresh and fragrant best come Christmas morning. We use them, like palms, to welcome the Messiah to our home. We use them, like olive branches, as signs of peace on earth.

Another Christmas Eve custom is not to eat. Instead, we give extra food to animals, including our pets and the birds in the backyard. On this night, if you can believe it, the animals join us in singing God's praise. Heaven and nature sing. And why not? With Mary and Joseph, the animals were the first to see the newborn Lord, who taught us:

Blessed are the pure in heart, for they will see God.

Hanukkah

Hanukkah begins on the twenty-fifth day of the Jewish month of Kislev and lasts until the second or third day of the Jewish month of Tevet. It lasts eight days in all. (Months on the Jewish calendar begin and end at the new moon. Because it takes 29½ days for the moon to pass through its phases from one new moon to the next, the months can be 29 or 30 days long.)

Days on the Jewish calendar begin and end at sundown. Hanukkah begins at sundown on:

December 23, 1997
December 13, 1998
December 3, 1999
December 21, 2000
December 9, 2001
November 29, 2002
December 19, 2003
December 7, 2004

Hanukkah can also be spelled Chanukah. It is pronounced *HAH-noo-kah,* but the initial "h" (or "ch") is aspirated as in the "ch" of the Scottish word "loch."

HANUKKAH

The Festival of Lights

The Jewish feast of Hanukkah begins about six days before the new moon of December. Because Hanukkah lasts eight days, on its first few nights the crescent moon shines in the east before sunrise. On its middle nights, the moon is too close to the sun to be seen. And on its final night, the "newborn" crescent moon shines low in the west in the evening sky.

Late autumn and early winter mark the olive harvest in countries around the Mediterranean Sea. Olives are an important source of oil used in cooking, in medicine and as fuel for lamps. During Hanukkah, doughnuts and potato pancakes (which are fried in oil), and other circular foods are like edible prayers for the renewal of the winter sun.

Candles are lit on each night of Hanukkah. One more candle is lit each night to drive away the winter darkness. They remind us of the enormous oil lamp—the menorah—that illuminated God's Temple in Jerusalem.

More than 2100 years ago, many people in Israel were giving up their Jewish culture for pagan culture. People stopped worshiping God in the Temple. To be fashionable, they even changed their names to make them sound pagan. But the family of Mattathias resisted. They stayed faithful to God and to God's law. Eventually the family rededicated the Temple to God's service and then celebrated for eight days.

The word *hanukkah* means "dedication" in the Hebrew language. Hanukkah is a celebration of faith in God, a faith that is dedicated and bright enough to resist whatever is evil in the surrounding culture.

Christmastime

Christmastime lasts from sundown on Christmas Eve until the feast of the Baptism of the Lord (on or around the second Sunday in January).

This second volume of *Take Me Home* has three handouts for the season — one about the Christmas tree, one about calendars, and one about gold, frankincense and myrrh. The first volume has three others — one about the "twelve days," one about the Epiphany blessing of the home, and one about the feast of the Baptism of the Lord.

Considering the commercial pressure to end Christmas once all the gifts are unwrapped, it is especially important for religious educators to do what they can to make the church's celebration of Christmastime familiar and appealing.

The take-home notes for Christmastime would be attractive on gold or green paper. (Notes duplicated on red paper can be difficult to read.)

CHRISTMASTIME

O Christmas Tree!

At the beginning of the Bible, in the book of Genesis, we read that God planted the tree of life in paradise. At the end of the Bible, in Revelation, we read that a new tree of life has been planted for us in the middle of heaven. God shines on the tree like unending sunshine.

Your Christmas tree can be for you a tree of life shining like heaven.

It's hard and messy to get the tree indoors and into its stand. You might want to do that one night and save the decorating for another night. Hanging ornaments is a task best done with time for reminiscing. To welcome the Savior, Christmas Eve is the customary night to light the tree for the first time.

Every evening from Christmas Eve until the Baptism of the Lord, gather around your tree to sing carols and tell family stories. Behave as if you are in paradise.

Each time you light the tree, enjoy how it dazzles the eyes. Then sing the following verse of "Hark! the herald angels sing":

Hail the heav'n-born Prince of Peace!
Hail the Sun of Righteousness!
Light and life to all he brings,
Ris'n with healing in his wings.
Mild he lays his glory by,
Born that we no more may die,
Born to raise us from the earth
Born to give us second birth.
Hark! the herald angels sing,
"Glory to the newborn King!"

Christmastime

The celebration of the new year is an important part of Christmastime.

In most cultures around the world, the harvest and the new year are two of the year's biggest festivals. But like most of our other holidays, we are turning New Year's Day into an ordinary work and shopping day. Let's try to buck that trend and encourage one another to recognize December 31 and January 1 as marvelous opportunities to rejoice in the Lord and in each other.

Beginnings and endings are holy times. For Christians, they can be signs of God's reign, where the past, present and future are rolled into one grand "now."

Unfortunately, religious educators are deprived of their students at the turning of the year. Perhaps the parish and parish school are wisely providing some wholesome New Year or other vacation-time gatherings for children and teens. Perhaps the new year and the ways it can be celebrated can be the subject of an Advent meeting or even a September meeting — other times of endings and beginnings that get rolled into one.

Fast Away the Old Year Passes!

Don't just throw the old calendar in the trash and replace it with a new one. Make a ceremony of the switch. When you take the calendar down, sit for a while with it. Thumb through it. Copy any information in it worth saving. If you're by yourself, reminisce about the year gone by. If you're with others, share a recollection.

Raise a glass of hot, buttered wassail, and offer a toast to old times. Sing "Auld lang syne." Then—if this can be done safely—indoors in a fireplace or outdoors in a barbecue grill, perhaps along with some dried Christmas greens, set fire to the old calendar. Let its smoke carry your thanksgivings and petitions to heaven.

Even if you can't burn the calendar, figure out a reverent and affectionate way to bid it adieu, perhaps by burying it in the earth or tucking it into a compost pile.

Now make a ceremony of carrying the new calendar across the threshold and into your home. (Perhaps until this moment you've kept it in the trunk of the car.) Welcome the new year, a newfound friend.

Like the great gift that a new year is, ornament the new calendar with flowers, ribbons and greenery. Flip its pages. When does Easter fall this year? What day of the week is your birthday? Are there any important anniversaries in store?

Bless the Lord for the gift of time. Ask the Lord for peace and prosperity for all the world. Hang the calendar with a rousing "hallelujah!"

Solemnity of the Epiphany of the Lord

Epiphany is celebrated on January 6. However, in most churches in North America, Epiphany is observed on the first Sunday after New Year's Day.

Epiphany is not the end of Christmastime. It is the high point. Christmastime ends on the feast of the Baptism of the Lord, and it even continues to echo until February 2, Candlemas.

"Epiphany" is hard to pronounce, but it deserves to be learned. Other titles for the day are "Twelfth Night" and "Three Kings' Day." The first volume of *Take Me Home* has a handout that explains the tradition of blessing the home this day.

In many ways, Epiphany is the most exuberant, most giddy feast on the church's calendar. The scriptures, prayer texts, chants and blessings of the Epiphany liturgy just about explode with superlatives, including the three gospel stories of the magi (from Matthew), the baptism of the Lord (from Mark) and the wedding at Cana (from John). It is a wonderful challenge for religious educators to share this exuberance with the parish at home, at worship and in class.

Among Roman Catholics in the United States and Canada, Epiphany is celebrated on the first Sunday after January 1. But in many other countries and churches it is celebrated on January 6, its ancient day, a day about which an old American song says "the stars in the elements . . . tremble with glee."

Distribute this take-home note during the week of January 1 or before Christmas vacation.

CHRISTMASTIME

The Gifts of the Magi

The second chapter of the Gospel of Matthew tells us about the magi who offered the Lord their gifts of gold, frankincense and myrrh.

Notice the sequence of events in this story. The magi spot a marvelous star. This sign in nature leads them to travel to Jerusalem, where they search the Jewish scriptures for an understanding of the sign. Now the scriptures — together with the star — direct the magi to travel onward to Bethlehem, where they find their hearts' desire.

This story tells us that God's creation and God's word together reveal Christ to us — and "revelation" is what the tongue-twisting word "epiphany" means.

Like the star, the gifts of the magi are signs from nature that are rich in scriptural meaning. Gold signifies royal splendor. The smoke of burning incense rises like our prayers to God. Bittersweet myrrh was used to perfume newlyweds and also to embalm the dead.

Our glittering and fragrant Christmas decorations, like the gifts of the magi, can be holy signs that remind us of the dignity of being a Christian. Make an Epiphany gift of one of these signs to someone who reveals Christ to you. Use chocolate coins for gold, a lemon studded with cloves for frankincense, or a pot of paperwhite narcissus for myrrh.

Incense and myrrh are resins, gooey liquids that drip from plants and then quickly harden. Look for them at religious goods stores or at an old-fashioned apothecary. When you heat them in an old pan, they will fill your home with sweet aromas.

Christian Unity Week
January 18–25

Christian Unity Week, which is actually an eight-day observance (an "octave"), is well-timed to occur in January, a month in which we celebrate the feast of the Epiphany as the ingathering of all peoples to adore the Lord.

A generation ago this week had more "steam" and was kept with enthusiasm. The various gatherings served the purpose of breaking down the walls of ignorance and distrust that stood between various Christian communities. Clearly, we still need Christian Unity Week.

How "parochial" (in the negative sense) is your school? Are its concerns self-directed or outwardly directed? How well acquainted do the students become with other expressions of Christianity? other religions? Are they being educated in religious history? Would they be able to identify what makes their own church unique and strong?

JANUARY 18 – 25

Christian Unity Week

Over the centuries, groups of Christians split into different churches. History shows that in many cases, there were good reasons for the separations. But in other cases the reasons now seem senseless.

Some churches want nothing to do with other churches. (And, again, there may be either good or senseless reasons for this.) But more and more churches are learning to cooperate. Cooperation starts with building up our knowledge of and respect for one another's differences. Every January, the separated Christian churches dedicate a week to prayer for unity. We pray in our Savior's words that "all may be one."

Get to know the history of a Christian church not your own. Visit other church buildings besides your own. Look for differences and look for similarities.

Almost every community will have opportunities for members of the various churches to gather this week in worship. All of us, no matter how we worship, can sing and pray the psalms together. Psalm 133 is perfect to learn by heart:

How good it is, how wonderful,
wherever people live as one!

It is like sacred oil on the head
flowing down Aaron's beard,
down to the collar of his robe.
It is like the dew of Hermon
running down the mountains of Zion.

There God gives blessing:
life for ever.

Feast of the Conversion of Saint Paul

January 25

If this feast falls on a Sunday, as it does in 1998, it isn't celebrated in the liturgy that year.

This handout makes note of the coincidence of two winter feast days that fall a month apart, the feast of Saint Stephen, the first martyr, and the feast of the conversion of Paul.

The murder of Stephen and the conversion of Paul are coupled stories told in the book of the Acts of the Apostles. "Martyr" means "witness." Stephen gave witness to Jesus, and this witness cost Stephen his life. Stephen saw the heavens open and "the Son of Man" appear. Paul too saw into heaven, and the experience blinded him until at last he came to faith and a new way of seeing. Of course, eventually Paul too became a witness of the Lord at the cost of his life.

These stories are told by the church in the month following Advent, as if to suggest some of the consequences of the coming of the Lord.

JANUARY 25

The Conversion of Saint Paul

In Jerusalem, after Jesus had risen from the dead and ascended into heaven, Stephen was killed because he was a Christian. Other Christians became afraid and fled to the city of Damascus. Saul set out to capture them. Suddenly, he was knocked off his horse and made blind by a brilliant light from heaven. He heard the voice of Jesus asking him, "Why are you persecuting me?"

For three days some Christians took care of Saul until he could see again. Saul began to live the Christian way of life and was baptized. He began to tell everyone that Jesus is the Son of God.

Saul was intelligent and used his talents to proclaim the good news of Jesus Christ. Saul took a new name, Paul, which means "short" in the Latin language.

On December 26 we celebrate the martyrdom of Stephen. On January 25 we celebrate the conversion of Paul. In between are the coldest days of winter. But soon afterward, the days quickly grow ever longer. The light gradually returns. Take some time to read about Stephen and Saul in the sixth, seventh, eighth and ninth chapters of the Acts of the Apostles.

At the beginning of his letter to the Galatians, Paul writes that it took many years for other Christians to trust him. After all, he once fought against the church. Throughout his life, Paul always seemed to be struggling with his faith and the right ways to express it.

Conversion to Christ may take just one shining moment, but it also takes a lifetime to grow steadily into this light.

Memorial of Saint Blase +316, bishop and martyr

February 3

This day is an optional memorial, which means that a parish may choose whether or not to observe it. If the day falls on a Sunday, it cannot be observed in the liturgy.

The blessing of throats on this day is fixed in Catholic memories. This blessing originated at a time when the calendar was filled with such saints' day blessings, when the year had many opportunities to bless the Lord in all sorts of ways for all sorts of reasons. Regardless of our affection for the blessing of throats on Saint Blase's Day, something got a bit skewed when this one blessing survived and the others got lost.

The good news, perhaps, is that these two volumes of *Take Me Home* (among other books, especially the church's *Book of Blessings* and *Catholic Household Blessings and Prayers*) have sought to revive, where appropriate, other seasonal blessings. This fuller picture puts today's blessing in context.

Use the day to teach about the church's sacrament of the sick. One understanding of this sacrament is that people with illnesses are themselves sacramental, "holy signs" of the love of Christ.

Saint Blase, Pray for Us!

Armenia is a beautiful country south of the Caucasus mountains, between the Black Sea and the Caspian Sea. Sixteen hundred years ago, Blase was the bishop of the city of Sebaste in Armenia.

A legend says that Blase lived for a while alone in the woods, like Jesus did when he fasted in the wilderness. Injured or sick animals came to Blase, and he would heal them. Another legend says that while he was bishop, Blase saved a boy from choking on a fish bone. Ever since then, people have prayed to Blase to cure illnesses, especially those of the throat.

On Saint Blase's Day in many parishes, people have their throats blessed. Two of the candles blessed on Candlemas (the day before) are tied in the shape of a cross and then touched to people's necks. The day falls in the middle of "flu season" and is a good reminder that we need to visit the sick and pay extra attention to anyone who is prone to get sick during winter.

When Christians are seriously ill, they celebrate the sacrament of the sick. Members of the church pray for healing and anoint the sick with oil. The fifth chapter of the letter of James in the Bible tells us to do this.

Too often we are embarrassed by illness. Or we stay away from sick people. But that is not the Christian way. Instead, we claim that sick people are beloved by God and by God's people. And so we lovingly touch their bodies with holy oil.

Caring for the sick is a sacrament, a sign of the mystery of God's love.

Carnival

Carnival is the festive period before Lent. Traditionally it lasts from Epiphany until the day before Ash Wednesday, a stretch of one to two months, depending on the date of Ash Wednesday.

Carnival is Christmastime's wilder sibling. Both times together were once the "holiday season" of the year, the customary time for all the imaginative ways people drive away their winter blues. This was the most likely time of year to learn a new dance, perform in a play or whip up a fancy dessert. Maybe this is still true of the winter season.

"Carnival" means "farewell to the flesh." These were the last days before Lent that Christian people ate meat and other rich food. Perishable foods had to be eaten before the warm weather of spring arrived.

The final day of Carnival is called Shrove Tuesday (because people were "shriven," or forgiven of their sins on this day) and Mardi Gras (which in French means "Greasy Tuesday," from all the fatty foods eaten on this day).

In New Orleans, customary Carnival colors are gold, green and purple — a merry mix that is used to represent the virtues of fortitude, faith and justice. The colors look backward to the gold, frankincense and myrrh of Epiphany and look forward to Easter, springtime and Lent.

Hand out the take-home note for Ash Wednesday during the week in which Carnival and Ash Wednesday fall. Hand out the note for Carnival the week before that.

CARNIVAL

Happily Ever After

Do you know what the name "Cinderella" means? It means "Ash Girl." Cinderella's relatives made her their servant. One of her jobs was to clean out the fireplace ashes. But thanks to the cleverness of her fairy godmother, Cinderella and the prince fell in love, and the story ends happily ever after.

This story is one of many stories that were told to cheer people up during the long winter nights between Christmastime and Lent. This in-between time is called Carnival.

Carnival together with Christmastime is really the Christian "holiday season"—or should we call it the "hospitality season"? With storytelling, singing and dancing, we help each other drive away the winter blues. We keep each other healthy.

Other Carnival stories include the tale of Pinocchio, whose name means "little pine tree," and of Rapunzel, whose name means "turnip root." The names are puns that remind us of some detail in the story.

The names of many characters in Bible stories are puns. It will take some study, but see if you can figure out why "Adam" means "earth," "Eve" means "life," "Isaac" means "laughter," "Deborah" means "bee," and "Jonah" means "dove." And what does your own name mean?

Like many Bible stories, Carnival stories teach us that things are rarely what they first seem to be. Before anyone can live happily ever after, the truth has to be uncovered and justice has to be served.

Purim

Purim falls on the fourteenth day of the Jewish month of Adar, which is one month before Passover. Like Passover, Purim comes at the time of a full moon and is a feast of liberation.

Purim begins at sunset on:

March 22, 1997
March 11, 1998
March 1, 1999
March 20, 2000
March 8, 2001
February 25, 2002
March 17, 2003

This feast is celebrated by a public reading of the Bible's book of Esther. True to this book's bawdy spirit, role reversal and masquerading have become a part of the holiday. So has charity to the poor so that everyone can celebrate together.

Emily Dickinson wrote, "A little madness in the spring is wholesome even for the king." Like the Christian Mardi Gras and Saint Patrick's Day, or like the first warm spell at the end of winter, Purim celebrations tend to get crazy. Clearly we have enormous human energy to channel at this time of year.

During Lent the church tells the story of Esther. It's one of several "paschal stories"—such as Creation, Noah and the Flood, the Exodus—that Jews and Christians tell in the spring, our time of "passing over."

PURIM

Stamping Out Injustice

The Bible's book of Esther is a very peculiar love story. Some of it is frightening and bloodthirsty, but most of it is funny and even ridiculous.

Here's a book of the Bible that is meant to make us laugh. You can read it in one sitting. It begins with a squabble between a haughty queen and a pompous king, and soon there's a beauty contest to find a new queen. It ends with the tables being turned once again as the wicked folks receive the evils they had intended for others.

When you read this story, keep track of how the plot shifts, especially in the ways that powerful and powerless people deal with one another. Their roles keep changing. The Jewish holiday of Purim is a celebration of this story. An important custom is to make sure everyone is able to take part. That's a good custom for any holiday.

At Purim the book of Esther is read out loud. One of the characters, Haman, is especially repulsive. He comes up with a scheme to destroy the Jewish people. So every time his name is mentioned, people shout and hiss and make a racket with noisemakers. They write his name on their shoes and then stamp their feet.

What's going on here?

In real life, unlike in this story, injustice isn't always punished. Wicked behavior wrecks lives. Sometimes in the face of evil all we can do is shout our disapproval and stamp our feet—and laugh, because the God of justice will have the last laugh, and oh, what a wonderful laugh that will be!

Lent

Lent is the season of preparation for Easter. Through fasting, prayer and charity (almsgiving) during the Forty Days of Lent, we prepare to renew our baptism at Easter. We prepare certain catechumens for baptism (who are now called "the elect" because they are chosen). And we lead people who have been alienated from the church back to their baptism and to unity with the church.

Prayer, fasting and almsgiving are lifelong disciplines that we renew every Lent. These disciplines are basic to the Christian way of life.

Naturally, these disciplines also are the customary ways by which the elect make ready for baptism and sinners seek reconciliation with the church. Everyone in the church is asked to pray, fast and practice charity in unity and in sympathy with the elect and with sinners.

The word Lent once meant "spring." It comes from the same root as the word "lengthen," because daytime lengthens during Lent. Dark winter passes over into bright springtime.

Ash Wednesday is the first day of Lent. (See the handout for that day in the first volume of *Take Me Home.*) Holy Thursday is the final day of Lent. The first four days of Lent, from Ash Wednesday until the following Saturday, are a kind of "warm-up" for the season, four days for making the transition from Carnival to Lent. The "Forty Days of Lent" are counted from the First Sunday of Lent (which is considered the "first day") until Holy Thursday (the fortieth day).

There are handouts in both volumes of *Take Me Home* for each week of Lent (and Eastertime, too), as well as this handout for the week of Ash Wednesday. Good paper colors for Lent include grays, purples, greens and buff brown.

Three Pillars of Life

Prayer, fasting and almsgiving are called the "three pillars" of the Christian way of life. They help support a full and healthy life. During Lent we try to repair and strengthen these three pillars, which also are called the "three disciplines" because they help people become better disciples of the Lord.

Prayer is conversation with God. Make a good habit of daily prayer. Read the psalms, and each Lent learn one or two by heart. Try to sing your prayer at home, and make every effort to sing well when you worship with others.

To prepare himself for his life's work, Jesus fasted in the wilderness. As Christians grow up, they need to learn traditional, healthy ways to fast. When we fast, we deny ourselves some food or other good thing. We remind ourselves of how dependent we are on God's gifts, which always must be shared fairly and never taken for granted.

Almsgiving means "sharing compassion." Almsgiving means more than giving away the things we don't need. It means giving away some of the things we do need because someone else also needs them. It means giving until it hurts.

Saint Augustine said that fasting and almsgiving are the two "wings" that help our prayers "fly to heaven." Prayer, fasting and almsgiving go together. They are ways we ask God to root out selfishness from our lives. They are ways we Christians live life to the full.

First Week of Lent

Liturgy Training Publications publishes a Lenten calendar, *Forty Days and Forty Nights*, which is a Noah's ark that sails toward Easter. Like an Advent calendar, there are windows to open each day.

Some sort of device for counting the Forty Days of Lent and the Fifty Days of Eastertime is a long-standing tradition, and you might want to keep the count posted somewhere in the classroom.

This business of what makes up the Forty Days of Lent has gotten confused (and is confusing). So here's an explanation: The "Forty Days of Lent" run from the First Sunday of Lent (the Sunday after Ash Wednesday) all the way through Holy Thursday, which is the fortieth and final day of Lent.

However, because Christians don't fast on Sundays, the Forty Days have only 34 fasting days. About 1400 years ago the church in Rome decided that in addition to the "Forty Days" there also should be 40 fasting days before Easter. The fast was begun on what we now call Ash Wednesday, to make 38 fasting days. Those 38 Lenten days plus the two fasting days of the Paschal Triduum (Good Friday and Holy Saturday) add up to 40.

A good classroom discussion might be to ponder how Jesus' 40-day fast in the wilderness ("among the wild animals," as Mark's gospel says) was like the flood in Noah's time and how both of those events can be something like what Lent is for us.

Forty Days and Forty Nights

The season of Lent begins on Ash Wednesday. But the "Forty Days of Lent" begin on the following Sunday, the first Sunday of Lent. The Forty Days end on Holy Thursday, when Lent ends. Count the days. They really do add up to 40!

Keep track of the count. A Spanish custom is to make a paper scorpion with 40 legs. Real scorpions should never be harmed, but this paper one represents the "sting of death" that Saint Paul tells us is punishment for sin. Each day of Lent, a paper leg gets pulled off, and at Easter the clawless critter gets tossed into the bonfire. In Christ, death itself dies.

Another way to count 40 is to create a paper bird each day, perhaps using *origami* paper, and hang it from a branch brought indoors. Or create paper or cotton-ball sheep and set them day by day on a green cloth or Easter-grass "pasture." By Easter you'll have a whole flock. Or make two animals each day and add them to a cardboard Noah's ark.

The number 40 reminds us of the 40 days of rain when Noah and his family and all those animals huddled inside the ark, which saved their lives. The number also reminds us of the 40 days that Jesus fasted and prayed in the desert before beginning his saving work.

During Lent we try to cooperate with one another, like the animals did aboard Noah's ark. We show God that we are ready for a new life. When the flood is past, the ark doors swing open, and God's rainbow joins earth to heaven.

Second Week of Lent

This handout explores the good habits of daily prayer. See this week in the first volume of *Take Me Home* for a handout about creating a place of prayer.

Parents and teachers: For splendid reflections on household rituals of nighttime and morning, check out Melissa Musick Nussbaum's books *I Will Lie Down This Night* and *I Will Arise This Day* (both published by LTP).

An Attitude of Gratitude

Ordinary days are filled with rituals. The word "ritual" means "repeated action." Most rituals come at the beginning and end of the day, in the morning when we wake up and at night when we go to sleep.

What are your morning and bedtime rituals?

Doing the same things over and over might sound boring, but we would quickly make ourselves sick if we skipped sleeping, eating, washing and showing kindness to one another. We can't have a healthy life unless we are careful about life's daily rituals.

That's one reason why every morning and evening is a time of prayer. Prayer keeps us healthy. Every day we give thanks to God. Every day we ask God to bless the world and all who live in it. Thankfulness and a concern for others are two "symptoms" of a healthy attitude.

If you can imagine this, we try to make every bedtime a rehearsal for our death and our judgment by God. And we make each morning a rehearsal for the day of resurrection.

During these weeks of Lent, Christians try to get back into the healthy habit of daily prayer. Talk this over in your family. Maybe you can sing your praise in the shower or while tying your shoelaces. Pray the Lord's Prayer when you make your bed each morning or when you turn the covers down each night. Your good-morning and good-night kisses can be acts of thanksgiving for the love that surrounds you.

Decide on some simple way to pray every morning and every bedtime, and then stick to it.

Third Week of Lent

When we think of Christmas our minds are flooded with images. That should also happen when we think of Easter, the richest of the Christian festivals — the "festival of festivals," as the church says, the festival that gives life and meaning to all the others.

How strong is your "Easter imagination"? Each year we have the season of Lent to reinvigorate our paschal vocabulary.

Many seasonal liturgical images rise out of the ordinary things we need to do. These human activities (many of them agricultural, such as breaking ground or sowing seed) are best accomplished communally, which makes them especially fine images of the communal life of the church.

This handout takes a look at one such necessary seasonal task — spring cleaning. Teachers might take some Lenten time to organize a "clean-up day" or two.

Spring Cleaning

The word "Lent" comes from "lengthen." In the Northern Hemisphere, the days get longer and the nights get shorter each day of Lent.

The extra sunlight warms the earth and cheers people up. But it also exposes dirt. It stirs the wind and blows dust and trash around. Sometimes the wind gets so strong that it breaks trees and damages buildings. It's no wonder that the month of March is named after Mars, the Roman god of battles.

Lent is spring cleaning time, and cleaning is an art! It takes a number of skills to learn how to clean something properly. Also, cleaning often takes teamwork and cooperation. We try to put aside our own selfish concerns. We try to work alongside others.

Before we clean a room, it is necessary to put things in their places. Start with your own things. You probably know better than anyone else where they go. And if you don't, ask someone. Figure out a system for keeping your things where they belong.

Washing windows is an art in itself, and it takes cooperation to do it safely. But nothing is more effective in brightening the home.

Clean outside, too. Pick up garbage, put clutter away, rake the yard and hose down the sidewalk. This is hard work. Maybe this spring you can help out a neighbor or a relative. Maybe you can be part of a group that cleans the outdoors.

This Lent you can help the sun, the wind and the rain give the earth its spring cleaning.

Fourth Week of Lent

The paschal language of the church is, at heart, the church's sacramental language. We might call it a "sign language"; it involves every form of human communication and every sense.

Once a year, at Easter dawn, the "signs" all seem to point in the same direction — straight into the kingdom of God. What are some of these signs? By Easter dawn, the days have grown longer than the nights. The moon has grown full. The first day of the week arrives. The sun rises.

Baptism, confirmation and eucharist, and the other rites of "christening" (literally, "making new Christs"), are also paschal signs — signs of "passing over." In ancient times in many churches, Easter dawn was considered the best time of all for baptism. Today, we too consider Easter and its holy eve the most fitting time for baptism.

But each parish is a bit different in its approach as the church keeps heightening its appreciation for Easter baptism and the rites that prepare for this event.

Teachers should get to know the parish catechumenate and especially the catechumens. Perhaps one of your own students or one of their relatives is a catechumen or one of the "elect" (the catechumens chosen for baptism this coming Easter). Their coming to faith is an amazing witness — and a "passover" — visible to all who seek deeper faith.

4TH **WEEK** OF **LENT**

Baptism, the Easter Bath

Easter Eve is the best night of all for baptism. No matter what day of the year you were baptized, Easter is its "anniversary." Baptism, like Easter itself, is a sign of the death, burial and resurrection of the Lord, a sign of the outpouring of the Creator Spirit.

Think about this for a while: Going into the water is like a death and burial. And coming out of the water is like a birth and resurrection, a new creation.

Baptism reminds us of the Bible's great stories about dying to an old way of life and being reborn to a new life. Three examples are the story of Adam and Eve, the story of Noah and the flood, and the story of the Exodus. And there are many, many others.

Some time during this Lent, read some of these stories in the Bible. Tell the stories from your own life that seem like endings and beginnings all at once. Ask about your baptism. Get to know the people in your parish who will be baptized at Easter. They are called the "elect" because they have been chosen. Pray for them.

During Lent, when we look forward to baptism, some people set up an empty bowl somewhere in their home, perhaps on the dinner table. Then at Easter they fill the bowl with water. To remember and to renew their baptism each morning from Easter Sunday until Pentecost, they take some of this water onto their fingertips to sign themselves with the sign of the cross:

In the name of the Father, and of the Son,
and of the Holy Spirit. Amen.

Fifth Week of Lent

At this point in Lent, everything in the life of the church should be geared up for Easter. Excitement and anticipation should be felt in every aspect of religious education. Put away anything that would diminish this excitement or distract from the coming of Easter.

What could be more destructive to a parish's liturgical life than for its organizations to schedule events that conflict with Good Friday, Holy Saturday and Easter Sunday? These are not the days for car washes, baseball games or band rehearsals.

An important goal of religious educators should be to foster children's attendance and thoughtful participation in the Triduum liturgies. Is there someone on the parish staff who can offer students and teachers a run-through of the Triduum?

This handout focuses on something fundamental — we can't even begin to participate in the Triduum unless we have freed up the time.

5TH **WEEK** OF **LENT**

Taking Time to Be Christ's Body

Sundown on Holy Thursday marks the end of the season of Lent. At that wonderful moment, we begin the Paschal Triduum, a tongue-twister of a phrase that means "the three days of Passover." The Triduum lasts until sundown on Easter Sunday. During these holiest days of the year, we celebrate the death, burial and resurrection of Christ.

Lent is a time to get ready for the Triduum. Before Holy Thursday, we try to get the house and yard clean, the Easter food and any new clothes bought, and the decorations up so that we can keep the Triduum free from distractions. If we have school, a game or a meeting scheduled for Good Friday, Holy Saturday or Easter Sunday, we do everything in our power to reschedule it. We don't want anything to get in the way of our time together.

Of course, there are some tasks that need doing even on holidays—such as caring for the very young and the very old. But no one needs to shop or entertain themselves during the Triduum. On Good Friday and Holy Saturday, leave the television and radio turned off.

Why do these days need our wholehearted attention? Over 1500 years ago, a man named Leo puzzled over the importance of the Triduum. Leo said that the body of Christ is our own body. And who could even think of being absent from their own death, burial and resurrection?

Imagine that. Without each and every one of us, Easter cannot happen!

Final Week of Lent

Holy Week is very strange. It begins on Palm Sunday with a "feast" of palm-waving in honor of the Passion of the Lord. (The first volume of *Take Me Home* has a handout about palms and their wonderful significance.)

The following Monday, Tuesday, Wednesday and Thursday (until sundown Holy Thursday) are the final days of Lent. These are customary days for cleaning, shopping, cooking and everything else that gets us ready to be free to direct our full attention to the Paschal Triduum, which begins at sundown on Holy Thursday.

The Triduum is not Lent. It is its own time, a three-day liturgical season. The Triduum is the heart of the year.

The final days of Lent, from Palm Sunday until Holy Thursday afternoon, are like the doorway into the Triduum, an entrance with Christ into the holy city of Jerusalem.

FINAL **WEEK** OF **LENT**

Ride On, King Jesus!

Our whole lives are like a procession. Sometimes we move from place to place, but always we are moving through time—until at last we march into eternity. Then our travels will be over. We'll be home at last.

The church celebrates this traveling by having processions. They're a way to pray with our feet! We have a procession on Palm Sunday. On that day we remember Jesus' entrance into the holy city of Jerusalem to keep the Passover. We too "enter Jerusalem"—at least in spirit—for our Passover festival, which begins Holy Thursday night.

An old song tells us that Jerusalem has twelve gates. Any kind of entryway—church doors, classroom doors or the front door to your home—can remind you of that great day when we will march with Jesus into the new Jerusalem we call "heaven."

A bunch of palms mixed with pussy willows and bright ribbons makes a good door decoration. So does a string of holiday lights. You might want to weave ribbons or strips of colorful fabric around the lights' electric cord. A wreath of flowers—a symbol of Jesus' Easter victory—is beautiful on a door.

A Russian custom is to leave doorways unlocked during the days from Easter to Pentecost. When Jesus died, his sorrowful disciples gathered in a room and locked the door. But when Jesus rose from the dead, he walked right through those locked doors.

Nothing can shut Jesus out, not doors, not locks, not even death.

The Paschal Triduum

The Three Days of the Death, Burial and Resurrection of the Lord

These three days, from Holy Thursday evening until Easter Sunday afternoon, are the Christian Passover. They are the most important days of the year. The Forty Days of Lent are a preparation for these days. The Fifty Days of Eastertime are kept in continued celebration of these days.

The Triduum is not too different from other human endeavors that unfold over several days, such as weddings, funerals and family reunions. There are quiet times, busy times and a "main event." The main event of the Triduum is the Easter Vigil.

On the day of a wedding, we can get so preoccupied that we lose our appetites. During the Triduum, this loss is called the "paschal fast." The fasting begins on Holy Thursday evening and concludes with the eucharist of the Easter Vigil—when the paschal "breakfast" begins.

How about initiating children into the proper spirit and the time-honored, wise and healthy ways that Christians fast? Jews (at Yom Kippur) and Muslims (during the holy month of Ramadan), as well as many Byzantine Christians, have long-standing ways of fasting—as well as ways to introduce children to fasting. Roman Catholics, too, have their traditions. What are these customs?

We have remembered much more about the ways to feast at Easter, and here the customs often reflect certain scriptural images: the paschal lamb, unleavened bread and bitter herbs, manna, the fatted calf. It's really not too hard to imagine a chocolate rabbit being, when all is said and done, a fine way to give ourselves a foretaste of "the land flowing with milk and honey."

This take-home note can be handed out along with the one for Palm Sunday or the one for Easter Sunday. Red, white and gold are colors associated with the Triduum. Perhaps you can also photocopy a song (with the proper permissions, of course!) for people to use at home during these holiest of holy days.

PASCHAL TRIDUUM

Easter Fast, Easter Feast

Have you ever been so emotional that you lost your appetite? Some brides and grooms get butterflies in their stomachs and have trouble eating the food at their own receptions. Because many mourners don't feel like eating, it's an old custom to tempt them to eat by bringing them a hearty meal.

On Good Friday and Holy Saturday, the Christian people lose their appetites. These are the days of the Easter fast. We keep any meals as sparse and simple as possible. We don't eat meat or other festive foods. We don't eat out, because we don't want to make anyone work on our holiest days.

In the presence of the cross of Christ—our tree of life—we pretend that we're in paradise. Only this time, we refuse to eat. We show God that we won't make the same mistake twice!

On Easter Eve, after the Vigil, the fast is over and the Easter feast can begin. Rainbow-colored eggs remind us of God's life-giving promise to Noah. Meats and sausages remind us of the paschal lamb that saved the people from slavery, of the fatted calf that Sarah and Abraham served to their guests, or of the calf served by the happy father when his prodigal son finally came home.

Sweet dairy dishes—cheesecake, eggnog and even chocolate bunnies—remind us that God has brought us home to a place the book of Exodus calls "a land flowing with milk and honey." In the words of Psalm 34, just taste and see how good the Lord is!

First Week of Easter

Easter Sunday is the third day of the Paschal Triduum. It is the solemnity of solemnities, the day of days, and it begins the Fifty Days of Easter, the happiest season of the church. The Fifty Days last until Pentecost.

This handout may be sent home with the one for the Paschal Triduum and perhaps with the one for the final days of Lent, too, especially if the students will not meet during the week. Schedule the distribution of these handouts so that there is time to prepare.

If this handout inspires you to organize egg-rolling or an egg hunt, keep in mind the timing of the White House custom — held on Easter Monday, not Holy Saturday. It would be decidedly anti-liturgical and untraditional to hold an Easter party before Easter Sunday. But the days of the Easter octave (from Easter Sunday through the following Sunday) are high holy days of the church deserving of all sorts of festivity. We want to make clear that these days are far from business as usual.

If the Easter octave is vacation time in your school, remember that we have 50 days for Easter celebrations.

The handouts for Eastertime would be attractive duplicated on pastel-colored paper.

1ST WEEK OF EASTER

Searching for Life

After Jesus was killed, his body was buried quickly. It rested in the tomb all through the sabbath, from Friday sunset until Saturday sunset.

Early on Sunday morning the women came back to the tomb. They wanted to embalm the body of Jesus with fragrant spices. But who would help them remove the stone that covered the tomb? Dazzling angels rolled the stone away! Luke's gospel tells us that the angels asked the women, "Why do you look for the living among the dead? Jesus is risen!"

Later that afternoon, a stranger walked with two of Jesus' friends along the road to the village of Emmaus. When they stopped to share a meal, the stranger made himself known. It was Jesus!

An Easter game called "egg rolling" is meant to help us imagine we are angels rolling the stone away from Jesus' tomb. While on their hands and knees, players use their noses (or spoons) to roll eggs across a lawn. The winner is the first to cross the finish line with an unbroken egg.

Egg hunts can call to mind the angels' words about searching for life. So could an Eastertime visit to a garden, a park, an arboretum, an aviary or a zoo. So could planting a garden and any of the ways we take care of the earth's creatures.

Outdoor activity during spring can remind us of Jesus' friends walking along the road to Emmaus. Whenever we hit the road, we had better be ready to see Christ in the people we meet.

Second Week of Easter

Eastertime is a 50-day-long season from Easter Sunday until Pentecost. This is the longest church season and the most ancient, too. Get to know it. Get to love it.

There's a lot to know and love about Eastertime. In addition to the wonderful signs we associate with Easter, these 50 days look like and have the feel of the many glories we associate with spring — first communions, Mother's Day, baseball games, May crownings, picnics, kite flying, handfuls of lilacs and apple blossoms and lilies-of-the-valley.

And in some years Eastertime includes many or all of the end-of-the-school-year activities.

Eastertime is a "week of weeks" plus a day — seven (days) times seven (weeks) plus one. Because seven in the biblical world meant fullness, the span of fifty days is a symbol of eternity. During Eastertime we "play heaven," living as if God's reign is fully here, as if the world were at peace and all people enjoyed lives of justice, good will and abundance.

Eastertime is a rehearsal for eternity.

2ND **WEEK** OF **EASTER**

The Waters of Life and Death

In Latin, Greek and Hebrew, the word for "wind" is the same as the word for "spirit." Other signs of God's Spirit are water, fire, wine, oil and fragrance. Why do things that are hard to grasp make good signs of the Spirit? During the Easter season we'll be discussing some of these signs. We start with water.

Read the first verse of the book of Genesis. *Before* the beginning, before God creates light or anything else, there's already an abundance of wind and water. Have you ever stood on a beach at night? Especially if the water is rough, it can be a frightening experience.

Other Bible stories remind us that sharp wind and deep water are a chaotic, deadly combination. The story of Jonah begins with a storm at sea. The next-to-last chapter of the Acts of the Apostles tells about Paul surviving a shipwreck.

Of course, even if water can drown us, all living things need it. The second chapter of the book of Genesis tells us that God made people out of water and earth. Then God planted a garden for us. A river kept it well watered.

Another Bible story that tells of water's power of life and death is the story of the exodus of the Hebrew slaves. God opened the sea so that they could escape to freedom. But then God closed the sea over their owners, who were trying to recapture them.

What else can water do? How is it used in your home? Float flowers in a bowl of water. Use this water to sign yourself each day with the sign of the cross.

Third Week of Easter

During Eastertime's 50 days, we're looking at some of the important sacramental substances of the church. This week we consider oil and fragrant chrism.

The story of Noah and the flood (chapters 6 to 9 in the book of Genesis) is essential (and delightful) reading during Lent, the Paschal Triduum and Eastertime. Besides offering us so much beloved liturgical imagery, the story provides several of the poetic images found in the Bible's Song of Songs and the book of Jonah. ("Jonah" means "dove" in Hebrew.) These scriptures are "flooded" with images of Christian initiation — paschal imagery.

In a sense, the Easter season is our release — from the ark after 40 days of Lenten rain, from the fish's belly after three days of the Paschal Triduum. We exult in a world grown green again. Our rainbow is the risen Christ, the sign of the promise of life. Our Beloved speaks to us:

> Arise, my love, my dove,
> and come away!
> For lo! The winter is past,
> the rain is over and gone . . .

When we're christened with chrism (a mixture of olive oil and the aromatic essences of flowers), we become new christs. We too become signs of the promise. Like Noah's dove, we become bearers of that marvelous olive branch, the token of reconciliation between heaven and earth.

Holy Oil

Nowadays we use oil mostly for cooking. We fry with it. We drizzle it on salads. We add it to dough to make baked goods light and flaky. Check out a supermarket to discover some of the many plants that produce edible oils. One oil-producing plant is the olive. Next time you eat an olive, notice that it's a bit greasy. That's olive oil.

Sometimes athletes are given a rubdown with oil to limber up their muscles. In the old days, oil was used to help heal burns and other injuries. Jesus' famous parable about the Good Samaritan (Luke 10:29–37) mentions how oil was used as medicine.

The church uses two different oils—one is to help heal the sick and the other is to rub on the catechumens, who are the people getting ready to be baptized. Catechumens are a bit like athletes, except that their struggle is to enter into the Christian way of life.

Besides the two oils, the church also uses a mixture of oil and perfume called chrism. Ask to smell your parish's sacred chrism. What other great fragrances does this Easter season bring to your neighborhood?

The word "christ" means someone who is anointed with chrism. We are anointed when we are baptized and confirmed. We become a new Christ. The holy name of Jesus becomes our family name.

Why is the perfume added? In his second letter to the church of Corinth, Saint Paul says that since dead things stink, a good smell can remind us of God's Spirit, the giver of life. People who are christened can share this life-giving aroma with everyone they meet.

Fourth Week of Easter

This week of Eastertime brings us an encounter with wax and the imagery of the beehive and the beeswax candle.

An Easter zoology lesson about bees is in order. So, perhaps, is a lesson about candle-making (and fire safety). Definitely required every Easter season is a class visit to the church to take a good, long look at the paschal candle and its symbolic decoration.

In most churches, this candle has five wax nails inserted in the form of a cross. The nails conceal grains of incense, which are symbols of the wounds of Christ. (Incense is the subject of next week's handout.) Like the risen body of Jesus, like any of us, this candle also has its wounds that give witness to God's love, which brings healing and is stronger than death.

In any classroom discussion of the sacramental signs of the church, make note of the scriptural mixing and blending that occurs. For instance, in reference to the perfume added to sacred chrism, last week's handout discusses Saint Paul's imagery of fragrance found in 2 Corinthians 2:14–16. This same imagery is part of the church's thinking about incense, and this thinking helps explain the use of incense as a symbol of the wounds of Christ.

In the mystery of the death, burial and resurrection of the Lord, even our death-dealing wounds have become fragrant (to cite Paul) with the aroma of life.

4TH **WEEK** OF **EASTER**

Beeswax

Have you ever seen a beehive? Many zoos have them in glass cases so that you can safely watch the incredible activity of the bees. Christian poets compare the church to a beehive, where everyone is supposed to work together for the common good. A beehive would fail if its motto were "every bee to herself." Individualism and selfishness wreck human society, too.

Special organs in the bees' bodies create the wax that bees use to build the hive. When you burn a beeswax candle, you're releasing energy gathered by the bees from flowers, which gathered energy from the sun. A candle flame is so simple and yet so amazing. It's also dangerous, like many other simple but amazing things.

Christian poets have written that baptized people are like shining candles. For a candle to burn, the wax must be burned up. Like a beehive, a candle is a sign of self-sacrifice, of the giving of ourselves for the good of one another. That's a reason Christians light candles during times of prayer.

In church during these 50 days of Easter, a huge paschal candle stands up front. We call its light "the light of Christ" and its flame "the fire of the Holy Spirit." The newly baptized receive their own candles lit from the paschal candle. These people are told to walk always as children of the light.

The paschal candle is like the pillar of fire that led the people out of their slavery in Egypt and onward to the promised land. Where is God's fire leading you?

Fifth Week of Easter

Eastertime lasts 50 days, a "week of weeks" from Easter Sunday until Pentecost. This is a good, long time that usually spans the near-final days of the school year.

As the weather warms and everyone gets antsy, think of the Pentecost story from the Acts of the Apostles: Under the prompting of the blustery Spirit, the disciples spill out into the streets. Walls cannot contain their energy.

The entire Easter season (and not just its final day) is a celebration of the Holy Spirit, poured out when Jesus died, poured out when Jesus rose from the dead, and poured out on the church whenever it gathers in prayer and praise.

Notice that the Spirit's pentecostal signs of noise, wind and fire are impossible to keep penned up or held down. So too are the sacramental signs of the church — such as water, oil, wine and smoke. What does that tell us about the nature of the sacraments?

This week's handout is about incense, which, like wax, is another potentially dangerous substance that requires a lesson on fire safety. Take this opportunity to show children the church's incense, censers and charcoal, and to talk about the whys and ways these things are used in the liturgy.

The story of the cloud filling the Temple in Jerusalem is found in 1 Kings 8:1–30. At the end of the story, King Solomon expresses what has become the church's cautious, paradoxical attitude toward its sacramental materials: "Will God indeed dwell on earth? Even heaven and the highest heaven cannot contain you, much less this house that I have built!"

Incense

Have you ever seen good incense? It looks like chunks of rock or beads of glass. Some incense looks like jewels.

What is incense? Certain kinds of bushes and trees have thick, gooey, sap-like substances called resins that drip from cut branches. Drops of resin dry and harden. Many resins have strong aromas, and some release their aromas when heated. These are used as incense.

You don't set fire to incense. Instead, you gently heat it until it melts, usually on top of burning charcoal. First the incense melts, and then it starts to smoke. Ask someone to show you the church's incense and how it is used.

For Christians, the smoke has many meanings. It rises heavenward, like prayer. It smells weird and wonderful. It surrounds us with mysteriousness, like the cloud that filled God's Temple. This cloud was so thick that the priests couldn't see what they were doing! Read about this cloud in the Bible's First Book of Kings, 8:1–30. Why do you think that something as fleeting as a cloud is a good symbol for something as eternal as the presence of God?

Most church-supply stores sell incense, or perhaps you can buy some from the parish. At your next family barbecue, give thanks to God by tossing some incense on the charcoal. Watch how the incense melts and smokes. Watch how the smoke curls and billows as it rises into the sky.

Sixth Week of Easter

If the students' understanding of "bread" is mostly limited to plastic-wrapped white bread, some consciousness-raising is in order. How about a trip behind the scenes at a bakery? How about gathering *panettone, challah, naan, pita, lavash* and other breads that show a wonderful range of sizes, shapes and flavors?

As background information for this and the next handout: Roman-rite Catholics use unleavened (yeast-free) bread for the eucharist. Byzantine-rite Catholics, in common with Orthodox Christians, use leavened (yeast-raised) bread.

Contaminated yeast is a scriptural symbol for corruption, and so unleavened bread symbolizes purity, a fresh start, a longing for "inspiration"—of the Spirit's pure "leavening."

Contaminated yeast makes a poor leavening agent. For the Byzantines, a well-raised loaf—which gives evidence that it has been leavened with uncontaminated yeast—is a symbol for the Holy Spirit enlivening the body of Christ as well as the Christian people enlivening the world around them—like fresh leaven in dough.

Eastern and Western Christians alike grace festivals with yeast-raised breads, often made richer with added fruits, nuts, eggs and cheese. It's hard to imagine a lovelier or more tasty symbol of the fullness and wholesomeness of the supper of the Lamb.

6TH **WEEK** OF **EASTER**

Bread

The word "companion" means "someone we share bread with." In communion, when we share the sacred bread and wine, Christ becomes our companion.

Have you ever made bread? If not, give it a try. But be warned: Making a yeast-raised bread will take many hours of waiting for the dough to rise. Yeast is a kind of fungus that slowly grows throughout the dough. Like any living thing, yeast gives off carbon dioxide. The gas expands the dough.

In the old days, people would keep a small lump of yeast alive in their kitchens by feeding it flour and water. Whenever bread was made, a bit was taken from the lump to add to the dough. But every so often other kinds of funguses would contaminate the lump and make it stink. When that happened, people threw it out and borrowed some uncontaminated yeast from a neighbor.

As a sign of new beginnings, every year at Passover the Jewish people get rid of anything yeasty in their homes. Passover bread is flat and "unleavened" (made without yeast). Our communion bread is unleavened, like the bread of Passover. Saint Paul said that stinky, contaminated yeast is like the rotten things we do. We should throw those things out and start fresh, like unleavened dough.

Christian poets have compared the Holy Spirit to fresh, pure yeast, but not the kind that makes dough rise. We're waiting for the day that the Holy Spirit makes the whole world rise!

Seventh Week of Easter

As holy communion in his body and blood, Jesus commanded us to "take and eat" and to "take and drink." It's strange how over the centuries we Christians have made excuses to skip the drinking.

Today, two emotional issues get raised in any discussion of communion from the cup: alcoholism and the transmission of disease. The first is a real, complicated and heartbreaking issue requiring the attention of every student, every educator and every parent. The second turns out to be a non-issue: According to plentiful evidence, sharing a common cup of wine is not a mode of transmission for disease.

Teaching an appreciation and a respect for wine is part of the upbringing of Christian children. We can start with the scriptures that speak of wine gladdening our hearts (Psalm 104:5) or making us insolent and prone to brawling (Proverbs 20:1). Tell about Noah and his vineyard (Genesis 9), about Esther's two banquets (Esther 5 and 7), about Belshazzar's feast (Daniel 5) and about the wedding at Cana (John 2).

7TH **WEEK** OF **EASTER**

Wine

Yeast causes bread dough to rise. Wine is also a product of the action of yeast, which is a kind of fungus. It turns the sugar in grape juice into alcohol, which eventually kills the yeast and stops the process.

The process is bubbly and sometimes even explosive. No wonder people once thought that "spirits" had invaded the juice! Christians think wine is a wonderful symbol for the action of God's own Spirit, who brings joy, honesty, friendship, unity—and great "explosions" of creative energy!

The alcohol helps keep the wine from spoiling. Nutritious foods with a long shelf-life—such as wine—were especially valuable in the days before refrigeration. But alcohol can make people intoxicated. Alcohol kills yeast and can kill people, too.

The Bible's book of Sirach (31:28–29) tells us that wine can inspire communion or conflict:

> *Wine drunk at the proper time and in moderation*
> *is rejoicing of heart and gladness of soul.*
> *Wine drunk to excess leads to bitterness of spirit,*
> *to quarrels and mumbling.*

Wine is one of many good things in life that can be used for harmful purposes. Learning how to put good things to good use is part of growing up.

The night before he died, Jesus shared a cup of wine among his disciples. He commanded them to do the same in his memory. This wine is Christ's blood, God's Holy Spirit, poured out for the life of the world.

Solemnity of Pentecost

Pentecost is the grand finale of Eastertime; it is the fiftieth and final day of the season. Pentecost is one of the greatest days on the church's calendar. Some of the day's traditional Jewish and Christian titles tell us how strange and wonderful Pentecost is: "festival of firstfruits," "the undoing of Babel," "the ratification of the covenant," "the giving of the gift," "the ingathering of the nations," "the full flowering of spring," "the marriage of heaven and earth."

Parents and other educators have the delightful responsibility to foster enthusiasm for a truly popular celebration of this splendid day.

In the first volume of *Take Me Home,* the handouts for the seventh week of Easter and for Pentecost include ideas for celebrating the Pentecost festival. This week's note in this second volume concludes our Eastertime-long exploration of sacramental imagery.

PENTECOST

Milk and Honey

Cows love fresh, green grass. Late spring must be their favorite time of year. An old English title for these days is "three-milk" because well-fed cows need to be milked several times a day. The result is that milk, cream, butter, cheese and yogurt are especially abundant in spring.

The Jewish holiday of Shavuot — 50 days after Passover — is celebrated by eating sweetened dairy dishes such as cheesecakes, blintzes and rice pudding. So is the Christian holiday of Pentecost — 50 days after Easter Sunday. Jews and Christians learned this delicious custom from one another.

Shavuot is a celebration of the people's arrival at Mount Sinai after their escape from slavery in Egypt. In fire and wind, God came down on the mountain to give the people their holy law. God promised that if they stayed faithful to this law, they would prosper in "the land flowing with milk and honey."

Pentecost is a celebration of the fiery, windy outpouring of the Holy Spirit on Jesus' disciples. In giving us the Spirit, Jesus keeps his promise to be with us until the end of time. If you can imagine it, Shavuot and Pentecost are like wedding days, promises of love and faithfulness.

All holidays need their once-a-year treats. Every Pentecost you can enjoy a taste of "milk and honey" by serving cheesecake for dessert. Topped with "tongues of fire" (in the form of burning candles), it's a traditional way to rejoice in the "birthday of the church" and the "wedding of heaven and earth."

Yom Hashoah, The Day of the Destruction

Twelve Days after Passover

Religious educators will have much work in making use of this handout. Before this day, search the newspapers for local gatherings that students can attend to remember the Jewish Holocaust. Most years bring articles and television programs in observance of this day.

If anything, organize a time of prayer and remembrance. LTP publishes *From Desolation to Hope: An Interreligious Holocaust Memorial Service*, by Rabbi Leon Klenicki and Dr. Eugene Fisher.

How good are you at introducing students to Judaism? *Teaching Christian Children about Judaism*, written by Deborah Levine and published by LTP, would be very useful.

Yom Hashoah falls early within the Christian Eastertime, which may be a fitting time of year — soon after Passover and soon after Good Friday. The Passover foods in stores and the coverage the festival gets in the press may help renew our awareness of and wonder about Judaism. Good Friday brings to the fore difficult and not-fully-resolved issues in the relationships between Jews and Christians.

Do not be afraid to deal with these subjects.

Yom Hashoah

A holocaust is a sacrifice offered to God that is set afire. In our own day, the word "holocaust" has taken on a terrifying significance. The word is used to describe the killing of the Jews of Europe by the Nazi government during the 1930s and 1940s.

This murder was very well organized and resulted in the death of over six million Jewish people (as well as millions of others: people who helped Jews, people with different political ideas, people with disabilities, and gay or lesbian people).

How could a government support such a horror? How could neighbors cooperate in the death of neighbors? And why didn't other nations put a quick stop to the Jewish Holocaust?

One of the reasons for this destruction—although it is only one reason—is that people lie to themselves. They don't want to face difficult and terrible things that occur all around them. They do not admit their own hatreds but instead make excuses.

Yom Hashoah, the day to remember the Holocaust and its victims, can be a day to renew the hard work needed to look at the world honestly and to act on what we see. We begin by learning what happened. How else can we keep history from repeating itself? We begin by remembering these people and the stories of their lives. We say "never again" to war and hatred and selfishness, and then we find ways to act on our convictions.

In prayer, in lighting candles and in singing psalms, join in this remembrance today.

Memorial of Saint George +303, martyr

April 23

By happy coincidence, Earth Day (first observed in 1970) falls the day before Saint George's Day — which might be called the "original Earth Day," since George is a patron of anyone who works the earth. His name in Greek means "earth worker" — a tiller of the soil. George also is a patron of springtime and the Easter season. He was martyred in the year 303.

The legends surrounding the lives of some saints are fantasy, not history. Learning how to interpret Christian folklore is a part of learning the Christian way of life. A good starting point in our interpretation is the saint's name, which offers strong clues to understanding how a legend can be understood as an expression of faith.

Like most legends, the one about George and the dragon is open to interpretation on many levels. For instance, perhaps the dragon represents winter, sin, death, our inner doubts, our addictions or any trouble that seems insurmountable. How good it is that along comes George!

APRIL 23

Saint George, the Dragonslayer

According to an old legend, there once was a gluttonous dragon who insisted that the nearby townsfolk bring it a hearty meal every day. When the food ran out (and it ran out quickly), the dragon said, "Your children look delicious." Ecclesia, the daughter of the king, bravely went to become the dragon's dinner. This was too much for George, so he slaughtered the dragon.

In time, Ecclesia and George fell in love and were married. Can you guess what they served at their wedding banquet?

Different versions of this wonderful old legend have been around for many generations. One version ends happily even for the selfish, overfed dragon. George doesn't kill it but instead teaches it to eat parsnips instead of princesses!

George was a farmer, which is what his name means — in Greek, "earth worker." Ecclesia's name means "the church." Saint George's Day is celebrated as an "Earth Day" for the church, a day to bless the Lord for gardens and farmlands and for the new life of springtime.

The one thing we know for certain about George is that he was a martyr, a word that means "witness." Martyrs give witness to Christ by dying for their faith.

Even this legend gives witness to the Christian faith, because whenever we are prepared to lay down our lives for one another, like Ecclesia and George, the dragon of selfishness is slain. The church gets a new lease on life. A royal funeral becomes a royal wedding.

Memorial of Isidore and Maria, husband and wife, farmers

May 15

This day has become a customary one for blessing farmlands. Like Saint George's Day and like the old Eastertime Rogation Days, today can be a celebration for the seed time and birthing time of the year.

In Spanish, "Isidore" is "Ysidro." Isidore's wife Maria Torribia was also declared a saint, "Santa Maria de la Cabeza," and so we may remember both of them on this day.

Isidore and Maria lived outside Madrid in the twelfth century. There's another Spanish Isidore on the church's springtime calendar, Saint Isidore of Seville, a scholarly and humble bishop who died in 636 and whose memorial is April 4.

MAY 15

Saints Maria and Isidore, Farmers

Spring is a critical time for farmers. Too much rain drowns the newly planted seed. Too little rain and the seed will not grow. A sudden frost, a windstorm or hail can wreck the crops and kill newborn animals.

Spring is a time of flowers, it's true. But it's also a time of fear, at least until the fledgling generation of plants and animals gets off to a healthy start. Keep farmers in your prayers during this season. Even if it means a long trip, visit farmlands as one way to give thanks to God for your daily bread.

Maria and her husband Isidore were farmers near the city of Madrid, Spain. They plowed the land every spring and sowed it with seed. They watched the orchards and vineyards bloom and grow fruitful. At harvesttime they gathered the crops and stored the harvest safely. They tended farm animals with kindness. No poor person who came to their door was turned away. Their farm was always a place of hearty and generous hospitality.

Maria and Isidore are the patron saints of farmers and farm communities. What did this couple do that was so saintly? Perhaps nothing extraordinary, yet in all the simple things of life, they gave thanks to God.

Blessed be God, the sun has risen! Blessed be God, the lilacs are in bloom! Blessed be God, breakfast is on the table!

Blessed be God for farmers on their feast day!

Memorial Day, U.S.A.

Last Monday in May

What has happened to this day? What used to be an occasion for mourning and remembrance has turned into one more shopping day.

This is not a Christian holy day but a national holiday. There's an obvious and serious danger in a church sponsoring a national observance, so parochial schools have to do some difficult balancing in the ways they teach students about Memorial Day. It doesn't serve the church to turn Memorial Day into another All Souls Day.

Memorial Day isn't and historically hasn't been a day for facile patriotism or for remembering all the dead; it began as a national day of reconciliation, a day for acknowledging that something in the nation is broken and in need of fixing.

One aspect of this day is the belief that people have struggled and died not for some "national interest" but in the cause of something that unites peoples and nations — "liberty and justice for all."

MEMORIAL DAY

A Day of Peacemaking

A civil war turns former friends and allies into deadly enemies. Different regions of the same country turn against one another. Workers in the same company might suddenly find themselves fighting each other. Even family members can turn into adversaries.

The hostility doesn't always stop after a war ends. How would you feel if someone who once tried to kill you moved into your neighborhood?

In 1868, soon after the end of the American Civil War, Memorial Day began to be observed not just as a day to remember people who died in the war but as a day to show and seek forgiveness, a day to begin rebuilding what war had destroyed.

We'll never stop needing that kind of Memorial Day. Make good use of this day. It can be much richer than simply a day to loaf or shop.

Visit a cemetery. Bring some flowers to decorate the graves of people you knew and people you didn't know. Visit a historical site. Learn about the Civil War and other wars. Ask to hear someone's stories about war, about being a refugee, about losing a loved one. To help us recall that this is a day of sorrow, top your flag with purple ribbons.

Make peace in your neighborhood if there's a conflict. Forgive someone who once harmed you. Repair something that's broken and make beautiful something that's ugly. Plant flowers. Plant a tree. Pray for justice, for peace, for healing and for reunion.

For the End of the School Year

The last day of school might not be the best day to send anything home, but perhaps a week earlier would be a good time to herald the end of the school year. That's just about all that students (and teachers, and administrators) can think about once the weather grows warm.

Take Me Home is a tool for Christian formation, a process that doesn't stop in summer. The season may be relaxed, but it's ripe with important holy days, important scriptures and important images of the paschal mystery. This book has several handouts for summer.

Even if your charge of students goes on hiatus, figure out a way to keep in touch: a monthly mailing? vacation Bible school? a parish-school picnic or day at the beach?

The school may want to sponsor summertime celebrations, and the two volumes of *Take Me Home* have more than enough ideas for those.

Building Bridges to Heaven on Earth

Ending any human adventure is an emotional moment. So is ending the school year. We may laugh or cry. We're saying farewell to our time with teachers and classmates. And we're suddenly a year older, even if it isn't our birthday.

As an old saying goes, "don't burn the bridges behind you." Instead, as the school year closes, build bridges of friendship by sharing extra kindness with everyone, talking to someone you may have ignored this year and asking forgiveness of someone whose feelings you may have hurt.

Size up the year gone by. List the accomplishments. Any regrets? Is it possible to repair what went wrong? How can you celebrate the good things that went right?

The approach of a vacation makes some people nervous. What will we do with the time on our hands? Putting our vacation plans in writing will help us organize our thoughts. It's hard to believe this in June, but September will be here before we know it. Make the most of summer vacation.

Some people think free time is a great symbol for heaven. There's an art to learning how to enjoy life in ways that help make the earth seem a bit more like heaven for everyone and everything on it.

Be sure to check out the vacation activities at the zoo, the arboretum, the planetarium, the natural history museum. In our summer recreation, we can be partners with God in re-creating the world.

The Summer Solstice

June 20 or 21

There's something off-kilter about inhabitants of the earth failing to grasp how the moon goes through its phases, how stars appear organized in constellations and how the daytime varies in length as the year goes by. But before we can really appreciate what causes these phenomena, we need to experience what they look like — yet because of street lighting, city dwellers may never get a decent view of a star-filled sky.

Why does this matter in our religious upbringing? Because the changes in the sun, moon and stars are part of the church's language of the paschal mystery, part of the poetic language we use to talk about and celebrate the gospel.

At times, religion class should include an astronomy lesson as well as a nighttime trip into the countryside to do some serious stargazing.

The solstice has been calculated down to the second, and that moment varies from year to year. In the late twentieth and early twenty-first centuries, the June solstice can fall on either June 20 or June 21. Interestingly, in the early years of the twentieth century, the solstice fell on June 21 or 22. (If those are the dates you learned as a child, you're showing your age!) In the years at the end of the twenty-first century, the solstice will fall on June 19 or 20. After 2100, the solstice again will fall on June 20 or 21. (This same sort of pattern is true for the other solstice as well as for the equinoxes.)

It takes just under 365¼ days for the earth to travel around the sun. So a leap year every four years accommodates the just-under-a-day that accumulates. This means, though, that every time a leap day is added, a little bit too much extra time is added. So about 400 years ago, mathematicians working for Pope Gregory VIII figured out a solution. They decides that century years should not be leap years unless they can be divided by 400. That means 1700, 1800 and 1900 weren't leap years, but 2000 is. This pattern also accounts for the three-day variation in the date of the solstice from 1900 to 2100.

It's no wonder students need so many courses in arithmetic!

Summer and Winter, Bless the Lord!

In winter and spring, the days grow longer and the nights grow shorter. In summer and fall, the nights grow longer and the days grow shorter. These shifts occur at the two solstices of the year, the one in late December and the one in late June.

"Solstice" means "sun stands still." For several days both before and after a solstice, the length of daytime stays about the same.

The summer solstice marks the longest days of the year, when the sun rises highest in the sky. Keep in mind that when it's the summer solstice in one hemisphere of the earth, it's the winter solstice in the other.

Christmas is a solstice festival. So is June 24, the birth of John the Baptist, and so is June 29, when we honor Peter and Paul, who made sure the church got off to a healthy start. July 1 is Canada's birthday. July 4 is the birthday of the United States. Why are the days around the solstice a fine time to celebrate births and other beginnings?

For generations, people have been celebrating the solstices with fire and light. Can you imagine why? While you're watching the evening fireflies, a rollicking lightning storm or a fireworks display, think a moment about your position on the earth as it wobbles on its axis and circles the sun.

Give thanks to God for bringing such order and change to the turning of the year. Give praise to Christ, the Light of the world.

Memorial of Saint Benedict +550, abbot and religious founder

July 11

Saints Benedict and Scholastica are patrons of Europe (along with Saints Cyril and Methodius). Benedictine monasteries are credited with preserving classical knowledge through the "dark ages," the years of chaos after the fall of the Roman Empire.

Benedictine communities also celebrate Benedict on his older feast day, March 21. But because a Lenten date isn't suitable for hearty celebration, July 11 became Benedict's memorial on the reformed calendar. Scholastica's memorial is February 10.

Do students know what you mean when you use the words "monk" and "monastery"? The words come from the Greek *mono,* meaning "one" or "single," an old word for hermit. Benedict's gift was to transcend individualism and establish healthy communities.

Like several other July saints, Benedict is a patron of travelers and of the hospitable treatment of guests. (See the handout for July 22, 25 and 29 in the first volume of *Take Me Home.*) Patrons of hospitality are good to have during the summer vacation season.

Saint Benedict of Nursia

Fifteen hundred years ago in Italy, the old Roman government was in chaos. The army broke ranks. The police stopped functioning. There was no one to protect people from bandits. Even the roads fell into disrepair, and markets quickly ran out of food.

What little food was left in the entire land was hoarded by the strong. Weak and sick people starved. This kind of selfishness turned neighbors against neighbors and destroyed families.

In these terrible times, a man named Benedict organized a community for men. His sister Scholastica did the same thing for women. Benedict put together a "Rule of Life," a very sensible set of guidelines for helping people get along and work together effectively.

The Rule said that greed, grudges, pride and laziness have no place in a community. Instead, everyone needs to work hard for the sake of one another. Generosity, forgiveness and charity are the only ways to bring order out of chaos.

Daily life was organized according to a Latin motto, *ora et labora,* "prayer and work." Any family can make that its motto too.

Benedict and Scholastica's communities thrived. New communities were begun. In our own day there are many Benedictine communities around the world. The Rule of Saint Benedict says that all guests are to be received as Christ, and so visitors are treated with great hospitality.

Saint Benedict's Day is July 11. Saint Scholastica's Day is February 10.

Elijah of Tishbe, prophet and wonderworker

July 20

Saint Elijah's Day is a major celebration on the Byzantine calendar and the most important in the month of July. It seems right during the heat of summer to remember the ninth-century BCE (before the common era) desert prophet who ascended to heaven in a fiery chariot.

The stories about Elijah are many and wonderful, but they are not very easy to find. They're scattered throughout the first and second books of Kings, beginning with 1 Kings 17, the story about the ravens feeding Elijah, and concluding with 2 Kings 2, the tale of the fiery chariot and the prophet Elisha receiving Elijah's spirit.

With children, you might make use of the lectionary for Mass, which divides the stories about Elijah into portions that are easy to read; see the first readings for weekday Mass, Year 2, for the tenth and eleventh weeks in Ordinary Time.

In cryptic passages in Matthew's gospel (11:14; 17:10–13), Jesus says that John the Baptist is Elijah! (According to Malachi 3:23–24, Elijah would return from heaven to herald the Messiah.) What do we have here? Scholars are undecided. It seems most everything about Elijah (and about John as well) is cloaked in rare and mysterious language that defies complete explanations.

Elijah, Prophet of Tishbe

The prophet Elijah was nicknamed "troublemaker." He stirred people up to believe again in God. Anyone who can't leave well enough alone will make enemies, so Elijah's enemies chased him into the desert.

While he was hiding, Elijah became so hungry that he wanted to die. Suddenly an angel brought him food. That gave him the strength to climb God's mountain. There was a great windstorm that cracked rocks, then an earthquake, and then fire. But God was not to be found in any of these. Then there was pure silence—and Elijah knew that God was there!

The stories about Elijah are found in the first and second books of Kings. The stories begin with the time ravens, not angels, brought Elijah his supper. They end with the story about Elijah traveling to heaven in a fiery chariot. We remember Elijah on July 20, during the fiery heat of summer.

Another prophet, Malachi, wrote that someday Elijah would return from heaven to announce the coming of the Messiah. Every Passover night, Jewish families open their door to welcome Elijah into their homes. He works wonders as he walks the streets to search for injustice and to set things right.

Celebrate Elijah's day by looking for ravens, by bringing refreshment to someone who is hot and tired or by rejoicing under the summer sun, which arcs across the sky like a chariot of fire.

Listen for God when the world grows silent. Open your door expecting miracles.

Memorial of Saints Anne and Joachim, parents of the Virgin Mary

July 26

Two issues may be raised by today's handout. One is that the scriptures sometimes contradict themselves, and this is something we ought to know. For a good example of contradiction among the four gospels, look over the accounts of Jesus' empty tomb.

A second issue is the church's remembrance of nonscriptural characters, such as Anne and Joachim, or nonscriptural events, such as the Assumption of Mary. Church reformers such as Martin Luther were not sympathetic to characters and stories that come from scriptural times but are absent from the Bible. The reformers felt that "scriptural silence" was to be respected.

That being said, devotion to the grandparents of Jesus seems natural and healthy. The names ascribed to these people come from the earliest centuries of the church. That the names have such rich meaning and are associated with scriptural characters are two clues that these nonscriptural figures had symbolic value for the early church and thus ought to for us, too. Perhaps they are idealizations of what Christians should be. We all need heroes.

The Grandparents of the Lord

Be sure to show your love to your grandparents on the day we remember the grandparents of Jesus. The gospels don't tell us about Mary's parents, but they do tell us Joseph's father's name. In fact, we're given *two* names! The gospel of Luke says Joseph was "son of Heli" (3:23). The gospel of Matthew says "Jacob was the father of Joseph the husband of Mary, of whom Jesus was born" (1:16).

Ancient writers provided names for the unnamed characters in the gospels. The centurion at Jesus' crucifixion was called Longinus, meaning "lance." The "good thief" who was crucified with Jesus was named Dismas, meaning "one who is dying." The Samaritan woman at the well was called Photina, meaning "enlightened."

Mary's parents were named Anne and Joachim. "Anne" means "gracious," and "Joachim" means "God raises him." Your own name probably has a meaning. It's worth learning and perhaps living up to!

Most names have variations. Some variations on Anne are Ann, Annette, Ana, Anita, Anna, Anika and Hannah. Legends about Saint Anne are a lot like the Bible's stories about Hannah, the mother of the prophet Samuel. These stories are found in the first few chapters of the First Book of Samuel.

Another biblical Anne is the prophet Anna, who spoke about the infant Jesus to all who were waiting for God to bring justice to the world. Read about her in Luke 2:36–38.

Lammas Day

August 1

If you've ever been to the very far north (such as to Alaska or Scandinavia), it won't be hard for you to imagine dividing the year into quarters according to the changing length of day. That's how the ancient Celts did it. The "season" that begins on May 1 and ends on August 1 is the quarter of the year with the longest days and the shortest nights. During the season beginning August 1 and ending November 1, the days rapidly grow shorter and the nights grow longer.

The liturgical calendar maintains vestiges of this way of dividing the year. Some of the old ceremonies of May Day (such as building a bonfire) are observed at Easter. Halloween, All Saints and All Souls are the way we have christened the first of November. Candlemas (February 2) and Lammas Day (August 1) reflect the other two turning points of the Celtic year.

This is not to say that the church took over "pagan" days: Instead, Christians recognize in the changing lengths of day (a change that is more dramatic the further we are from the equator) a sign of the paschal mystery, the mystery of our "passing over," our transfiguration in Christ.

AUGUST 1

Lammas Day

Have you ever seen "amber waves of grain"? Few sights on earth are as spectacular as a field of ripe wheat rippling in the wind.

The wheat harvest takes place in summer. The people of Israel celebrate it at *Shavuot,* also called Pentecost. Ukrainians begin the harvest on June 29, the feast of Saints Peter and Paul. Years ago, the Celtic people celebrated the harvest on August 1—called "Loaf-mas Day," shortened to "Lammas." The "loaf" was the bread baked from the first harvested wheat.

To celebrate this most important harvest of the year, people decorate doorways with "harvest crowns," large wreaths made out of straw. These are easy to make or to find in stores.

Making "corn dollies" is another harvest custom. The word "dolly" here means "image." "Corn" can mean any kind of grain. A corn dolly is any sort of construction woven out of straw. It takes the form of a person, a cross, a spiral, even a royal scepter.

Rejoice in the summer harvest! Make a "Lammas Day" for yourself by giving thanks for the produce from your own garden or from a farmer's market. Stop by a roadside stand to buy basil, peppers and okra. See if there's a place where you can pick your own sweet corn, peaches or muskmelons.

Break an especially fine loaf of bread tonight. Say these words from Psalm 147: "Hallelujah! The Lord fills our land with peace, giving us golden wheat."

Feast of Saint Lawrence, deacon and martyr

August 10

There are very few saints' days ranked "feasts," but today is one of them, which shows the importance of this day. (Most of the days that we call "feasts" are actually classified on the church's calendar as "memorials." "Feasts" are usually reserved for celebrations of the Lord and Mary.)

The name "Lawrence" means "bay laurel," the evergreen shrub that is used in cooking and was once used to fashion the leafy crowns that adorned the heads of athletes and heroes. In Greek, the crown itself is called *stephanos,* which gives us the name of the other great deacon-martyr, Stephen, whom we remember on December 26.

The days of many of the church's ancient martyrs — such as Lawrence, Stephen, Cecilia, Lucy, Agnes, Polycarp — have accumulated a wealth of folklore and traditions, many of them revolving around the time of year and the agricultural cycle. This folklore borrows freely from even more ancient sources, some Jewish and scriptural, some pagan.

These folktales and traditions have been preserved by the church in its daily prayer, the Liturgy of the Hours. For instance, the old antiphons for evening prayer and morning prayer on St. Lawrence's Day remind us about Lawrence calling the poor "the church's treasury" and about the legend of his martyrdom on a fiery gridiron (an image of August's often oppressive and sometimes deadly heat) — although this legend doesn't quite agree with what we now know about the persecution of Christians by the Roman authorities.

You can't appreciate the folklore if you get preoccupied with what really happened and expect the lives of the saints to read like history lessons. Sometimes what's required is to sit back and enjoy a tall tale, a yarn spun around a campfire, a story that makes us groan or chuckle or sends shivers down our spines.

There's a reason why Jesus told so many parables in proclaiming the gospel.

AUGUST 10

A Servant of God

Wish people named Laura and Larry a happy feast day on August 10, the day we remember Deacon Lawrence of Rome. One of the customary tasks of deacons — "deacon" means "servant" — is to help share wealth fairly among members of the church.

A legend says that Emperor Valerian's police ordered Lawrence to hand over the church's money. Lawrence pointed toward people who were poor or in slavery. He said, "These are the wealth of the church." The police were so angry that they chained Lawrence to a gridiron and hung him over a fire.

Because of his horrible martyrdom, several customs began for remembering Lawrence on his feast day. One custom is to eat cold foods and offer folks a refreshing break from the summer heat. You might serve ice cream, go swimming or check up on people who have trouble dealing with heat.

Another custom is to have a barbecue as a way to ridicule Emperor Valerian and anyone who causes great suffering. "Lawrence" means "bay laurel," a plant woven into victory crowns, which became the emblem for all the church's martyrs. So spice your supper with bay leaves.

Beginning tonight and peaking in the early morning hours of August 12, the sky sheds what are called "tears for Saint Lawrence" — the Perseid meteors. These meteors radiate from the constellation Perseus, in the northeast sky, close to easy-to-find Cassiopeia, which looks like the letter "W." On a moonless night you may spot a meteor every minute.

Solemnity of the Assumption of the Virgin Mary into Heaven

August 15

This day is the most important festival of Mary. It is her "Passover," her death, rest and resurrection. Assumption may have once been celebrated with a night-long vigil in mourning for the death and burial of Mary followed by a day of celebration for her resurrection.

One title for the day is "Dormition," meaning "falling asleep." The title "Assumption" describes Mary's being raised up by Christ into God's eternal life.

Popular celebrations of the day are titled "Our Lady of the Harvest," "Our Lady of the Sea," "Our Lady of the Sky," "Our Lady of the Hills." All created things are blessed today in the raising of one of God's creatures into glory. Thomas Merton wrote, "It is my own sister, my own flesh and blood who is assumed into heaven!"

In *To Dance with God,* Gertrud Mueller Nelson reminds us of the linguistic connection between the words "matter" and "mother." The Mother of God and all mothers are gifted by the Creator with creative power. The earth's August fruitfulness can be seen as a reflection of this sacred creativity.

Catholic Household Blessings and Prayers includes an Assumption Day blessing of garden produce. The handout for this day (and another one in the first volume of *Take Me Home*) can set the tone for this liturgy. Blue or gold would be appropriate colors for the paper.

AUGUST 15

The Passover of the Mother of God

On the night of August 14, Assumption Eve, the church gathers to keep vigil. The woman who gave birth to Christ is entering into her "passover," her "transfiguration."

In the heat of this summer night, we surround a statue or picture of Mary with August flowers. We keep watch. We pray. We wait. There is tremendous mystery in passing over!

On the morning of August 15, as the sun rises, we tell the good news: "All honor to you, Mary! Today you were raised above the choirs of angels to lasting glory with Christ!"

A beautiful legend says that after Mary died, the apostles gathered near her tomb to mourn. But the tomb was open, and Mary's body was gone. The tomb was filled with herbs, flowers and fruits, the bounty of a summer garden.

Assumption Day is a time to bless the Lord for the fruitfulness of the earth, sky and sea. Nearly the world over, Christians rejoice in Mary's Assumption by getting into the great outdoors—to hike, to swim, to cloudgaze, to have a picnic.

To celebrate this day, bite into a ripe peach and let the juice drip down your chin. Crumble oregano, basil and rosemary over your evening meal, and inhale the aromas. Rise early and caress a dewy lawn to get some heaven-sent "holy water" on your hands, and then bless yourself with the sign of the cross.

Like our Blessed Mother Mary, we too will die, rest, and rise in the glory of Christ.

Memorial of the Martyrdom of Saint John the Baptist

August 29

There are 40 days between August 6, the feast of the Transfiguration of the Lord, and September 14, the feast of the Holy Cross. In some places, these 40 days were once a kind of penitential season leading to the autumnal change of seasons.

Fasting at this time of year came naturally. Who had time for fancy meals when there was so much work to do in putting up the harvest? That communal work — like any activity done for the common good — became a sacramental sign of the church itself.

The muggy, buggy days of late summer will always be a time for eating light, keeping tempers in check and shifting gears as vacation days turn quickly into the busy-ness of September.

In the middle of these 40 days comes the remembrance of the death of John the Baptist, a day which remains a fasting day on the Byzantine calendar. Western Christians probably need more such days of sorrow. We have too few on our calendar, and there's no lack of sorrows to face.

This handout will need to be coupled with a reading of the gospel account of the death of John (Mark 6:17 – 29) and a discussion of this puzzling event, which raises the issues of the abuse of power and the senselessness of tragedies.

AUGUST 29

A Day of Mourning

Steamy summer is winding down. At night the katydids click-click-click to call for their mates. The cicadas wail in the treetops like sirens, as if something serious is about to happen.

Back when summer began, we joyfully celebrated the birth of John the Baptist. He grew up to announce the arrival of Jesus. John's father said that Jesus would shine like the rising sun.

Now, at the tail end of summer, we remember John's death on August 29. John was thrown in prison and then murdered by King Herod. This frightening story can be found in the sixth chapter of Mark's gospel. For the king and his court, John's beheading was nothing but a party prank. For us, John's death was a tragedy. We remember it by observing a day of sorrow.

One way to keep the day is by eating simply and skipping meals, treats and entertainment. This is called fasting. Sorrowful people usually don't feel like eating. How do you react when you are sad? By fasting, we show solidarity with people who are sorrowful.

How do you try to help people who are sad? One way to show concern is simply to drop what we are doing and go to be with them. Sometimes all we can do is sit in silence, and that is enough.

Keeping a sad day is hard but good. Being sorrowful in sympathy with others who are sorrowful is a blessed and necessary task. Jesus tells us, "Blessed are those who mourn, for they will be comforted."

For the Beginning of the School Year

Perhaps we should try to make the beginning of the school year a big deal. There's much worth celebrating. There's energy to direct.

The school no doubt has some celebration and orientation planned, but what happens in the home?

A Rite of Passage

Can you imagine throwing a party because school is back in session? Why not? There's plenty to celebrate when people have a chance to grow in knowledge, literacy and experience.

In Russia, the first day of each school year means flowers for teachers and sacks of candy for students. In India, the students themselves are decked with flowers. In Israel, honey cookies are baked in the shapes of letters of the alphabet.

We have our back-to-school rituals, too. Some families make alphabet soup for supper. Some turn a September weekend into a celebration of learning: They visit a museum or historical society or take a tour of a book or newspaper publisher. The buying of school supplies, gym clothes or new shoes is a "ritual" that takes place in almost every household.

Make a big deal of these everyday things. Spread a table with a cloth. Around it, gather the family. On it, gather the new things that will be used at school. Thank the Lord for bringing you to this powerful new beginning. Talk about your hopes and fears for the new school year.

This passage from Psalm 78 seems perfect for this moment:

Let future generations learn
and let them grow up
to teach their young
to trust in God,
remembering great deeds,
cherishing the law.

Memorial of Our Lady of Sorrows

September 15

The first volume of *Take Me Home* has a handout for September 14, the feast of the Holy Cross. It is one of many handouts for September. This month is rich in take-home notes because it acts like a "new year" holiday. September needs its rallying cries for so many parish and parish school endeavors.

Holy Cross Day is such a cry. In monastic tradition, Holy Cross marks the change from warm weather to cool weather; Good Friday marks the change from cool to warm. These two days are poles in the calendar.

The memorial of Our Lady of Sorrows is a continuation of the feast of the Holy Cross.

The Sorrows of Mary

September 14 is the feast of the Holy Cross. On September 15 we join with Mary, who bravely stood close to her son Jesus as he was dying on the cross. We call Mary "Our Lady of Sorrows."

"Dolors" is an old word for sorrows. So this is the name-day of anyone named Dolores. We remember seven dolors of Mary:

1. Hearing the prophecy of Simeon that "a sword of sorrow" would open her heart.
2. Fleeing into Egypt with her family to escape King Herod's plot to murder her baby.
3. Losing the twelve-year-old Jesus in the Temple in Jerusalem.
4. Seeing Jesus carrying his cross.
5. Witnessing the death of Jesus, when the sun went dark and the earth itself shook with sorrow.
6. Receiving Jesus' dead body in her arms.
7. Burying the body of Jesus in the earth.

In a mysterious way, these are the sorrows of every person who follows Jesus. We too must open our hearts in living our faith. We too must be willing to lose what we love most. We too must give witness to suffering. Like our Blessed Mother, in sure and certain hope of the resurrection, we too embrace and then bury the bodies of those who have died.

Gladioluses bloom in abundance in September. This flower's sword-shaped leaves give it its name, from the Latin word for sword, *gladius*. In remembrance of Simeon's words to Mary, use them to ornament the holy cross today.

Jonah, +8th century BCE, prophet

September 22

Saint Jonah's Day is observed on the Byzantine calendar, which includes the days of the prophets as well as other figures from the Jewish scriptures.

The book of Jonah is proclaimed in synagogues on Yom Kippur, the Day of Atonement, which is a day of fasting. Jewish poets see Yom Kippur as especially well timed because it falls close to the equinox, the day on which daylight and darkness are equally balanced. This balance is a classic image of the moment God first created the world. Some say the vernal equinox is the anniversary of creation, some say it is the autumnal equinox, and some say both moments bring us back to the beginning.

The book of Jonah, like the Day of Atonement, deals with the restoration of the equilibrium of heaven and earth, of nation with nation, of person with person.

Christians can recognize parallels with the liturgical year. The 40-day fast of the Ninevites (which included the town's animals) is for us an image of Lent. Jonah's three-day stay in the fish, as well as Jonah's three-day journey through the town, are images of the Paschal Triduum.

SEPTEMBER 22

A Big Fish Story

The people of Nineveh lived selfishly. So God told Jonah to go and warn them to straighten out their lives, or else they would face dire consequences! But Jonah thought the people weren't worth saving, so he got on a ship that sailed away.

A sudden storm threatened to capsize the ship and drown everyone on board. Jonah knew he was the reason for the storm. So he begged the sailors to throw him into the sea. No sooner did he hit the water than a huge fish swallowed him alive.

That's how the short book of the prophet Jonah begins. Read how it ends. The book is filled with puns and poetry. Jonah's name is itself a pun. It means "dove," which is our clue to compare Jonah's story to the story of Noah's dove (found in the eighth chapter of the book of Genesis). Both Jonah and the dove set out on journeys over water, and even though their first missions fail, their second missions bring the promise of a new way of life.

Some people ask if the story of Jonah is true. It's probably wiser to wonder instead how the story is filled with truth.

We remember Jonah at the autumnal equinox, when day and night reach a balance, each twelve hours long. The sun rises due east and sets due west.

A grand old way to celebrate a day of equilibrium (and to usher in the autumn season) is to fast, like the people and even the animals of Nineveh. Then make a donation to a food bank so that your fasting can become someone else's feasting.

Rosh Hashanah and Yom Kippur

Because Jewish days begin and end at sunset, the Jewish holy days begin the evening before these calendar dates:

Rosh Hashanah, "The Head of the Year"

October 2, 1997	September 18, 2001
September 21, 1998	September 7, 2002
September 11, 1999	September 27, 2003
September 30, 2000	September 16, 2004

Yom Kippur, "The Day of Atonement"

October 11, 1997	September 27, 2001
September 30, 1998	September 16, 2002
September 20, 1999	October 6, 2003
October 9, 2000	September 25, 2004

The turning of summer into autumn brings what might be called the "Jewish holiday season," which spans 23 days. First comes Rosh Hashanah, at the new moon that inaugurates the seventh month of the Jewish calendar. Ten days later falls Yom Kippur, the holiest day of the year.

Five days after that, at the full moon, begins the seven-day Sukkot festival. (A handout about Sukkot is found in the first volume of *Take Me Home.*) Then comes Sh'mini Atzeret, which "sets the seal" on the festival period and ushers in Simhat Torah, a day for "rejoicing in the Law." Simhat Torah brings its own ending-and-beginning: The final words of Deuteronomy are proclaimed (about the death of Moses, which concludes the Torah), and then come the first words of Genesis: "In the beginning . . ."

These many days are treated in some detail in LTP's *Companion to the Calendar,* by Mary Ellen Hynes.

Renewal and revitalization are "themesongs" running through the Jewish High Holy Days. So are the images of harvest, of completion and new beginning, of assembling the people and of forgiveness, peacemaking and reconciliation.

We Christians should resist reformulating these days to fit our own agendas. Instead, we might join with our Jewish neighbors in some of their celebrations, perhaps at a Jewish community center and especially at home.

ROSH HASHANAH

To a Sweet New Year!

In the Jewish calendar, months run from one new moon to the next, a period of about 29½ days. That's what the word "month" once meant—or should we say "moonth"? The first month of the Jewish year comes in spring, when the world seems reborn.

Seven is a sacred number, so the seventh month of the Jewish year is filled with sacred days, beginning with Rosh Hashanah, which comes at the new moon when the month begins. This day is the Jewish New Year. (That's right—the Jewish year begins with the seventh month.)

In synagogues this day, the shofar—a ram's horn—wails with its wonderful, eerie sound to call the people together. On Judgment Day, the Messiah will sound the shofar loudly enough to wake up the dead!

Rosh Hashanah is the annual anticipation of Judgment Day. According to tradition, God opens the book of life and begins to write down the names of those who live justly and mercifully. Ten days later, on Yom Kippur—the Day of Atonement—God stops writing, and the book is sealed shut. Throughout these ten "Days of Awe" people greet one another with the words, "May your name be inscribed for life in the book of life!"

Circles and spirals are emblems of time and eternity. Begin supper on Rosh Hashanah by sharing a round loaf of bread. You might be able to find or bake the spiral holiday bread called hallah. Core an apple and slice it in circles. Dip a slice in honey and give thanks to God for a sweet new year.

Memorial of Saint Thérèse of the Child Jesus +1897, religious

October 1

She is known by many names. Baptized Marie Francoise Martin, she entered the Carmelite monastery at Lisieux and received the name Thérèse of the Child Jesus.

From her writings (in which she promised that after her death she would plead with God to "let fall a shower of roses," in other words, blessings), she's also known as the "Little Flower."

Some aspects of people's affection for the Little Flower have been superstitious and self-centered. But her popularity is deserved. She is an advocate for the immeasurable wonder of ordinary life. She reminds us that selflessness, humility and cheerfulness in the routine acts of life take enormous courage.

September 30, 1997, is the centenary of Thérèse's death.

Spring-flowering bulbs are planted in early autumn. They can go most anywhere that receives sunlight in springtime, except in soils that get waterlogged in winter.

Most kinds of bulbs will put on a good show the first year after planting. Daffodils and other narcissus have a better chance of returning year after year than do tulips and hyacinths. Many kinds of small bulbs — snowdrop, crocus, chionodoxa, squill, windflower — can multiply over the years to cover a large area.

Plant the larger bulbs six to ten inches deep, the smaller kinds about three inches deep.

OCTOBER 1

The Story of a Soul

Marie Martin's sisters joined the Carmelite convent in their town of Lisieux in France. Of course, Marie wanted to be with them, so she too became a nun—when she was only 15 years old! She received a new name, "Thérèse of the Child Jesus."

Some of the nuns were stern with Thérèse and gave her the worst chores. They didn't want her to be spoiled. It takes humility to live as a Christian.

The words "humility," "humble" and "human" come from the root-word "humus," the brown, crumbly material in soil. The book of Genesis tells us that God created the first human out of the earth. So being humble requires knowing what we are—but we're more than dirt. Genesis tells us that God breathed life into our bodies. In the Bible, another word for "breath" is "spirit."

Thérèse performed even the most boring and nasty chores with a loving and cheerful spirit. She made her work a kind of prayer. Her joy re-created the spirit within her community.

At age 24, Thérèse died of tuberculosis. Her life had been brief and ordinary, but while she was sick, the nuns asked her to write about it. Her writing is called *The Story of a Soul*. People find this short book an inspiration to live less selfishly and with more appreciation for the holiness of a humble life.

On Saint Thérèse's Day, plant spring-flowering bulbs in a dry, sunny spot. Though these bulbs too are humble-looking, they are filled with the spirit of life. Come Eastertime, they will rise in glory.

Memorial of St. Teresa of Jesus +1582, doctor of the church

October 15

On October 1 we remember Thérèse of the Child Jesus, a French Carmelite nun who died in 1897. On October 15 we remember her namesake, Teresa of Jesus, a Spanish Carmelite nun who lived in Avila during the sixteenth century.

These are the years when Martin Luther labored to reform the church in Germany. Teresa was also a reformer, and, like Luther's, her ideas were attacked by people in power.

Times change. In 1970, her scholarship earned her the title "doctor (wise teacher) of the church." But most of Teresa's efforts were aimed at reforming the Carmelite way of life, not the church as a whole.

Teresa's was a tremendously appealing and complicated personality. She might be considered the patron of anyone who is romantic, ecstatic, witty, sharp-tongued, scholarly or spoiled rotten but then experiences a change of heart. She took Mary Magdalene and Augustine as her patrons.

A recipe for Saint Teresa's bread and for *yemas de Santa Teresa* (not really for children to try because it involves hot sugar syrup) can be found in Evelyn Birge Vitz's wonderful book *A Continual Feast,* published in 1985 by Harper and Row.

Saint Teresa of Avila

Teresa liked fancy clothes, expensive perfume and juicy gossip. She read trashy romance novels. And she was a nun! Her convent was really a social club for spoiled, rich Spanish girls.

But as she grew older, something happened to Teresa, slowly at first, to change her attitudes. She was smart, and she had always been impatient with the opinions of narrow-minded people. She knew that acting like a Christian would mean using her brain.

Teresa struggled to begin a new community where the women would try to live the Christian way of life. They would pray, fast and give charity to those in need. But Teresa was never a stick-in-the-mud. She loved to dance, and she clicked castanets while she sang. Even if she was the boss, she worked alongside others as an equal.

Teresa became friends with John of the Cross, a scholar and poet who shared with Teresa a love for scholarship and simplicity.

Teresa fasted from meat, and so milk and egg dishes are eaten on her feast day. Celebrate the day with meatless Spanish foods such as *yemas de Santa Teresa*—cinnamon and lemon-flavored nougat candy—or make Saint Teresa's bread, which is French toast flavored with cinnamon and lemon and then fried in olive oil.

Saint Teresa once said, "The Lord lives among pots and pans."

Saint Ursula and Her Companions, third-century martyrs

October 21

Nothing certain is known about Ursula and her companions. This day was once a very popular saint's day, but it is no longer observed on the Roman calendar. Although Saint Nicholas remains on the calendar, nothing certain is known about him, either. There is a rather long list of saints who enjoy great popularity and whose stories are legends, not history.

Not only do we not know anything factual about Ursula, the church has a long history of *admitting* that we don't know anything about her! A ninth-century sermon says that nothing about the woman can be verified but then goes on to recount the legend in detail—because a good story is more than facts, and a gospel-soaked legend can bring us close to truth.

Ursula is regarded as a patron of dance the way Cecilia is considered a patron of music. Heavenly patrons of the arts are good to honor, especially as the cultural calendar gets back into full swing each autumn. Saint Ursula's and Saint Cecilia's days can be like pre-winter pep rallies for the arts.

OCTOBER 21

Saint Ursula and Her Companions

An old legend tells the story of Ursula, a Christian princess from Britain. Her father had ordered her to marry a non-Christian prince, and she was miserable about this. So she escaped with ten girlfriends. (Some versions of the legend say it was with 11,000 friends!) They set sail and traveled down the Rhine River to the city of Cologne, Germany.

The tribal chieftain of the Huns fell in love with Ursula. She refused him, just as she had refused the prince. In his fury, the chieftain murdered her and her companions — all except one, a girl named Cordula, who hid herself. But the next day she mustered her courage and came forward to join in her friends' fate.

Dancing had been their favorite pastime. So now in heaven, they hold hands and circle around the throne of the Lamb of God. They praise God by dancing.

Saint Ursula's Day is a herald of Halloween, All Saints and All Souls, when we begin to muster our own courage to face the winter. We'll need to hold tightly to one another if we are to make it safely through that often depressing and sometimes dangerous season.

As nights grow long, we welcome one another into the firelight. We dance and sing and tell tall tales, including the family stories that can get more and more fantastic (like the legend of Saint Ursula) as the years roll by.

In spirit, we join hands and begin the heavenly dance that will reach its crescendo at Christmas.

October 31, November 1, November 2

All Hallowstide

All Saints Day is one of the premier days of the church, certainly the greatest day on our autumn calendar. Halloween is not a separate celebration; rather, it is the beginning of All Saints, the holy eve of the festival. November 2 (and on through the month) continues the celebration.

Keep All Saints and All Souls with Halloween traditions. Work hard to recognize in the familiar customs and decorations of Halloween evidence of Christian faith, of hospitality and generosity, of a healthy remembrance of the dead in anticipation of the great homecoming of heaven.

Don't believe what you read about Halloween being a "pagan holiday." People the world over hold harvest festivals and days to remember the dead. Beginning on the evening of October 31, we Christians hold a harvest festival, our festival of ancestors, a feast of the paschal mystery clothed in autumnal robes.

Religious educators will want to prepare October 31 and November 1 and 2 with care. Plan activities that will bring parish children and youth together with the other generations.

The first volume of *Take Me Home* has three take-home notes for these days: one for Halloween, one for All Saints and one for All Souls. These notes were written for parochial school students. The note in this second volume has a very special audience in mind: trick-or-treaters!

ALL HALLOWSTIDE

Trick or Treat

For over a thousand years, many Christian people have been celebrating their greatest autumn festival on November 1, All Saints Day. The festival begins the night before, on Halloween, and continues through November 2, All Souls Day, the day of the dead.

This is an important time of year for celebration. All at once it seems that leaves color and fall, gardens get frosted and birds depart. Something holy, wonderful, mystical, and, at times, also very sad seems afoot.

All Saints is a harvest festival, and so we celebrate with pumpkins, apples, mums and bright autumn leaves. Jesus told us that God's angels will gather us into heaven just like farmers gather the harvest into their barns. We'd better not be weeds!

Halloween, All Saints and All Souls together are a festival of the dead. We remember our ancestors with affection. We dare to imagine what lies on the other side of the grave. Death is terrifying, yet we make fun of it with goofy skeletons and ghosts. In Christ we will have the last laugh, even over death.

Dressing up in costumes and going begging may seem like a weird way to celebrate the saints, but think about it: Nobody deserves heaven, yet by God's good grace — God's own hospitality — heaven is open to a surprisingly motley crew of the poor, the lowly, the hungry and thirsty, the sorrowful and the persecuted.

These are Jesus' own words: Blessed are the pure in heart, for they shall see God.

Memorial of Saint Martin de Porres +1639, religious

November 3

It's amazing how sympathetic a figure is Saint Martin de Porres! He's considered a patron of ecologists, of those who work for interracial justice, of social workers and of anyone whose mystical sensitivity to nature leads them to deeper patience, kindness and a heightened sense of justice. A hero of the Americas!

His feast day is well timed in this holy month of November and, in connection with All Saints and All Souls, might be a starting point for the ingathering of clothes, food and other material goods for distribution at Thanksgiving. In this month of remembering the dead, bear in mind that the most traditional memorial is sharing and practicing charity.

In south and south-central climates, early November is an excellent time of year for another traditional way to memorialize the dead: planting trees. And that, too, is a tradition for Saint Martin's Day. Martin planted orchards to feed the hungry and taught people to preserve and cultivate trees.

NOVEMBER 3

Saint Martin de Porres

No one wanted to clean the toilets, so Martin did that, and he did it cheerfully. He also fed the animals and took care of the gardens. His favorite work was caring for people who were sick. In art, he's often shown with a broom, tending a sick person or playing with his pets.

Martin de Porres lived as a Dominican brother in the city of Lima, Peru. His fellow brothers thought he was a pain in the neck. Martin let homeless people sleep in their house. He planted fruit trees in their yard to feed the hungry. Then he opened a home for children who had been abandoned by their parents.

When Martin was a baby, his own father abandoned him. His father's people were from Europe, but his mother's people were from Africa. Anyone whose parents come from different heritages has a patron in Saint Martin de Porres.

He may have been difficult to live with, but the people of Lima fell in love with Brother Martin. They came to him for advice when they had fights, when they were sick and when there was trouble in their homes. Martin always seemed to know what to do.

November 3, Saint Martin de Porres's Day, is perfect for doing as Martin did: cleaning the house cheerfully, making sure the hungry have something to eat and the lonely have someone to talk to, planting trees, showing sympathy for animals, negotiating arguments and making peace.

Feast of the Dedication of the Lateran Basilica in Rome (324)

November 9

This feast is ranked so highly that we celebrate it even when it falls on a Sunday, as it does in 1997 and in 2003.

Why the high rank? The Lateran Basilica is the "mother church" of Roman Catholicism. It—not the Vatican—is the bishop of Rome's (the pope's) cathedral church.

The Lateran Basilica was dedicated first to the Savior and then to John the Baptist, and so the feast was called the "Dedication of Saint John Lateran," a title that is terrifically confusing. But this is not a confusing feast. The dedication day of any church is an occasion to celebrate the community that worships there. So today we celebrate the Roman Catholic Church.

Your own parish and diocese have their anniversary solemnities too. If the day isn't known, the Sunday before All Saints can be observed. The dedication day of a church is really a kind of All Saints festival, a festival to anticipate where we're headed on our journey toward judgment and (God willing) glory.

Take some time in November to retell the history of the parish and the diocese. Explore the church building. Some have "consecration crosses" and candles that mark where the walls were anointed with chrism, as if the building itself had been christened by the Holy Spirit. Maybe you're lucky enough to know and to celebrate your dedication and consecration days.

The school building, too, has its dedication anniversary. Does this happy event have its annual renewal?

This handout makes reference to 1 Kings 8 and 1 Corinthians 3. The reference to "living stones" is from 1 Peter 2:5.

Living Stones

At first, Christians worshiped in one another's homes. That worked just fine until more and more people were baptized.

In the year 324 in the city of Rome, the emperor gave Christians a large public building on Lateran Hill to use for their Sunday gatherings. On November 9 they dedicated it to Jesus, their Savior. The building is called a basilica, which means "fit for a king," because it is so large and roomy.

Each year the church remembers the anniversary of the dedication of the Lateran Basilica. This building is the cathedral parish of the bishop of Rome, the pope. (The word "cathedral" comes from the Latin word for the bishop's chair, *cathedra*.)

Do you know the history of your cathedral? Do you know the history of the buildings of your parish? Take a trip if necessary, and do some exploration of these places. And what about the history of your home? It too is a worthy place for prayer.

King Solomon built God a fabulous temple. On its dedication day, the king said that if heaven cannot hold God, then neither could this temple.

Christians get nervous when someone says that one place is holier than another. We think everywhere on earth is holy. As much as we love and need our beautiful buildings, we know that baptized people are the "living stones" that build up the church. Christ is our sturdy foundation.

Memorial of St. Margaret of Scotland +c.1093, married woman

November 16

Memorial of St. Elizabeth of Hungary +1231, married woman, religious

November 17

Margaret was born in 1046. Elizabeth was born in 1207. These two different women had much in common. Both were intelligent and born into royal families. Both married rulers and so became queens. Both spent portions of their lives in exile to escape enemies (in Elizabeth's case, her in-laws). Both were very well loved by the citizenry for their care for people in need. Both died young and worn out.

And after they died, both became patron saints of their nations, patron saints of married people and of family life, and patron saints of those who assist anyone in need.

Such patrons visit the church in its collective memory just when they are most needed, as the weather turns mean and as the family reunions and charity drives of the late autumn and winter holidays are being prepared.

NOVEMBER 16 AND 17

Noblesse Oblige

Because of war in their native England, Margaret's family escaped to Hungary. From there they moved to Scotland, where King Malcolm fell in love with Margaret. He was a roughneck and a bully, but he learned from her how to love others. They married and became famous for their hospitality and fairness.

Elizabeth was born in Hungary. When she was still very young, her family arranged that she would marry Prince Louis. They sent her to be raised by Louis's family in Germany. Luckily, Louis and Elizabeth grew up to love one another very deeply.

The trouble was that Prince Louis's family hated Elizabeth's generosity to the poor. But when they complained, Louis always stood up for his wife. Tragically, the prince died young. His family threw Elizabeth out of their home. Now she and her children were poor. She too died young; she was only 24 years old.

Margaret and Elizabeth had much in common. They were wealthy, noble women who learned what it was like to be poor and homeless. They had happy marriages. They had many children. And they are called saints because of their unselfish love for people in need.

Remember them by gathering clothing, food and money for the needy, by making peace within the family, by loving people despite their flaws and by helping your home be a place of generous hospitality to guests.

Noblesse oblige: "Nobility has its demands." God calls those who have been given much to give much.

Memorial of Saint Cecilia +3rd century, martyr

November 22

Not much is known about Cecilia or even why she is the patron of music. But the church needs its musical patrons in heaven and on earth.

Schools too need patrons of the arts. What a terrible tragedy it is when music programs are gutted because budgets are tight, as if music was expendable, as if learning the musical arts wasn't essential to a healthy soul.

The church says that music is essential to worship. The attitude that music might be nice but is not necessary to worship is contrary to the church's liturgical law. In observing the spirit of this law, the church takes its cue from its first and best hymnal, the Book of Psalms.

NOVEMBER 22

Singing Saint Cecilia

It's smart to be afraid of the dark, because unless you can see where you're going, it's easy to stumble and fall. In November the days are short and are getting shorter. Fearful thoughts creep into our minds: What would happen if the sun stopped shining and night lasted forever?

Then along comes Cecilia, the patron saint of music. She tells us to cheer up! If you're afraid, then whistle in the dark. Sing by yourself or with others. Practice an instrument. Listen to music. Attend a concert.

Jesus once told a story about ten bridesmaids who waited one night for the groom to come to his wedding. Five were wise and kept their lamps burning brightly. Five were foolish and let their lamps burn out.

Some Christians like to think of Cecilia as the first of the "five wise bridesmaids" who brighten this dark time of year. Next comes Saint Lucy on December 13. Even her name means "light." Then there's Saint Agnes on January 21 and Saint Agatha on February 5.

Who's the fifth wise bridesmaid? It is the Blessed Virgin Mary, who teaches us best how to shine even when we're afraid and even when we grow anxious and expectant.

A month from today is the winter solstice, and then comes Christmas. That's when the whole church will sing out with Mary and Cecilia and all the saints these words from Psalm 96:

A new song for the Lord!
Sing it and bless God's name,
everyone, everywhere!

Thanksgiving Day

Second Monday in October in Canada,
Fourth Thursday in November in the United States

The people who first "invented" the observance of Thanksgiving Day were seventeenth-century Puritans who centuries earlier had done away with the Roman Catholic liturgical year. As late as the early years of the twentieth century, there were New Englanders who refused to keep Christmas and made Thanksgiving the great family festival of the year.

Today Thanksgiving is kept by most Catholics as if it were a holy day. We need a harvest thanksgiving on the calendar. Among European Catholics, Assumption Day, St. Michael's Day, All Saints Day and St. Martin's Day (and other occasions) have been or still are harvest festivals.

In crafting Thanksgiving, the Puritans made use of customs that European Catholics would have associated with St. Martin's Day or Jews with the festival of Sukkot. We Americans really can rejoice in several long-standing aspects of the holiday: the emphasis on unity and reconciliation captured in the folk tales of the cooperation between Native Americans and settlers, as well as the feasting on native American foods.

Those amazing and yet now common foods were unknown in Africa, Asia and Europe before the time of Columbus. Those foods—especially maize and potatoes—were responsible for the great boom in human population that followed their introduction into European and Asian agriculture.

Lately, Thanksgiving has come under the threat of being engulfed by the commercial imagery of "the holidays." In the past few years in the United States, more and more stores have decided to open on this day. But they wouldn't be doing this unless enough people wanted to spend Thanksgiving shopping. What's going on here?

The first volume of *Take Me Home* has a complementary handout for Thanksgiving as well as a handout for the Sunday before Advent.

THANKSGIVING

Now Thank We All Our God

The Pilgrims may have been a serious and hard-working people, but they loved their songs. Their homemade music made happy times happier and made sad times more profound.

From morning to night, turn Thanksgiving into a feast of song. Sing at suppertime. Sing after supper. When you get sleepy, sing sleepy songs. To rouse yourself, sing rousing songs.

The day is blessed with a cornucopia overflowing with songs: "Come, ye thankful people, come," "We gather together," "Let all things now living," "My country, 'tis of thee," "Sing to the Lord of harvest," "We plow the fields," "O God, our help in ages past," "All people that on earth do dwell." (And let's not forget "Over the river and through the woods"!)

If you don't know the words, hum or whistle the melodies. Or, with the help of a hymnal, get ready a few days earlier and make songsheets. Talk musicians into bringing guitars, recorders, violins or harmonicas. Begin with a single, simple song:

Now thank we all our God
with hearts and hands and voices,
Who wondrous things has done,
in whom this world rejoices;
Who, from our mothers' arms,
has blessed us on our way
With countless gifts of love,
and still is ours today.

For Celebrating a Birthday

Here's a note to send home on birthdays.

The "creepy" birthdays mentioned in this note are found in Genesis 40, 2 Maccabees 6 and Mark 6. It is in fact very odd — and noteworthy — that the Bible seems so indisposed toward birthdays. Since only the rich and powerful knew and celebrated them (and forced their subjects to celebrate them), they seem to be occasions that focused the people's resentment toward their rulers. We can sympathize if we've ever taken part in a birthday party for a spoiled child.

Perhaps this notion might spark worthwhile discussions about our obligations as gracious hosts on the big days of our lives, our birthdays, graduations and weddings. Explore the difference between accepting being spoiled on those occasions and expecting to be spoiled.

The custom of the birthday cake is one of several that express domestic communion. We learn best how to offer eucharist by learning how to share family meals in grace and gratitude. Oddly, the birthday cake (like a birthday itself) is a customary *memento mori,* a reminder of death. One of these days our candles will get blown out for good!

All such reminders are meant to hone our values and sharpen our appreciation for the things that really matter. In the meantime, we make our wishes and share with our companions the sweetness life offers.

CELEBRATING **A BIRTHDAY**

Happy Birthday to You!

The three birthdays mentioned in the Bible turn out creepy. After his birthday celebration, Pharaoh strangled his baker. King Antiochus was a lunatic who celebrated his birthday every month. As a party prank at his birthday, King Herod beheaded John the Baptist.

Why do the scriptures tell us only weird stories about birthdays? Perhaps because long ago the only people who celebrated them were royal and rich. Ordinary folks didn't have calendars, so they couldn't keep a record of when their children were born.

The Bible does have some wonderful stories about births, though. Everyone knows the story of the birth of Jesus (Luke 2:1–20). But do you know the just-as-wonderful story of the birth of John the Baptist? See Luke 1:5–25, 57–80. Read about Hagar giving birth to Ishmael (Genesis 16:1–16), about Sarah giving birth to Isaac (Genesis 18:1–15; 21:1–8) and about Hannah giving birth to Samuel (1 Samuel 1:1—2:11).

The story of your birth, too, is a wonderful story, and your birthday is a perfect time for telling it or hearing it told every year. Be sure to write the story down. Keep adding details as you discover them.

In some ways, a birthday can be like the eucharist. We gather with others in love. We tell the stories of how we came to be. We cheerfully give and receive gifts. In sharing a common food—a sweet foretaste of heaven—we give thanks to God and offer our praise.

For Those Who Are Sick

Here's a note to send home when someone's sick — for those times when we experience ordinary colds and sniffles and other unpleasant but not life-threatening illnesses.

The text makes reference to several gospel passages: the healing of the man born blind (John 9), the anointing with oil (Mark 6:13), the laying on of hands (Mark 16:18), and the question on Judgment Day about our care for the sick (Matthew 25:26). The text also mentions a passage from Isaiah, 33:24.

FOR THE SICK

Get Well Soon!

The prophet Isaiah wrote that God's reign will be a place where nobody gets sick. No wonder we ask God, "Thy kingdom come"!

Some people think sickness is God's punishment, but Jesus said that this is a ridiculous way to think. Being sick isn't a sign of God's anger, and being healthy isn't a sign of God's blessing.

Jesus said that on Judgment Day, when we will be called to account for our lives, God will be angry not if we got sick but if we didn't visit and care for the sick. God will be gladdened if we did.

Some people think it's smart to stay away from sick people. But that goes against Jesus' instructions: Members of the church should visit the sick and touch them with affection, pray with them, and, when it's right, anoint their bodies with oil—like the Good Samaritan did to the man who was beaten up by robbers.

People who have become ill are especially near and dear to Christ and to the church. We say that these people can be "sacraments"—holy signs—who bear in their own bodies the sufferings of Christ.

When you get sick, remember that you can be one of God's holy signs. Try not to be grouchy, stubborn or uncooperative. You might write down what your sickness feels like. Those feelings can be quickly forgotten once you're better, but they are good to remember during the times you care for someone else who is sick.

For Those Who Are Moving

Here's a note to offer when someone moves away or moves into a new place.

The story of the expulsion from paradise is Genesis 3. The tale of the first journey of Abraham and Sarah is Genesis 12. The short book of Ruth comes early in the Bible, after the books of Joshua and Judges.

MOVING TO A NEW HOME

Moving Day

It's fun to move to a new home. It can be scary, too, and sad, and it's hard work. We need to help one another. We especially need to keep our spirits up.

Probably the worst move of all was when Adam and Eve left Paradise. Ever since then, no matter where we live, we carry inside ourselves a bit of homesickness. One day, God willing, we'll make it to our final and best home, the heavenly city, the new Jerusalem.

God told Abraham and Sarah to move from their hometown to a new place. What a move! They had to travel on foot along with all their sheep, cattle, donkeys and camels. Imagine having to walk to your new home.

Naomi and her family moved to Moab from their hometown of Bethlehem. But then a terrible thing happened: Naomi's husband and sons died. She told her daughters-in-law to go back to their parents, but her daughter-in-law Ruth insisted, "Don't ask me to leave you! Wherever you go, I will go. Wherever you make your home is my home as well. Your people will be my people, and your God will be mine." And so, in love, the two women traveled back home to Bethlehem.

Moving days emphasize what matters most—not things or even homes, as holy and good as they are. What matters most is our loyalty to and our love for one another.

When we move, we can link arms with our family and make Ruth's words our own, "Wherever you go, I will go. Wherever you make your home is my home as well." That can be our blessing as we say farewell to the old home and as we greet the new one.

For Those Who Mourn

The story of the death and burial of Sarah is found in Genesis 23. The story of Abraham's death and burial is found in chapter 25.

Jesus' saying about the grain of wheat is John 12:24. The image of Christ as the firstfruits of the dead is from 1 Corinthians 15:20–26, which is proclaimed on Assumption Day, the "harvesting into heaven" of the Blessed Virgin.

Blessed Are the Dead

When Abraham's wife Sarah died, he bought a small plot of land to bury her body. Her grave was the very first piece of the Holy Land.

Our graves also are pieces of the Holy Land. We bury the dead in the earth, carefully covering them with it as if they were the grains of wheat that Jesus spoke about. On Resurrection Day they will rise, like a harvest, "to bear much fruit."

The scriptures call Jesus "the firstfruits of the dead." Jesus is the first to rise, but there will be another harvest, and another, and another, until everything that has died comes alive. May that day come soon!

Abraham's sons Ishmael and Isaac had always been rivals, but when their father died, they came together in affection and peace to bury him next to Sarah.

Funerals have always been times for family reunions. Resurrection Day will also be a reunion, the happiest one ever. And, if you can imagine this, every Lord's Day we rehearse it! Around the holy altar we gather in communion with the living and the dead.

These are the church's own words about the last and best Lord's Day of all, when death itself will die:

On that day we shall see you, our God,
as you are.
We shall become like you
and praise you forever through Christ our Lord.